THE WAR
I ALWAYS WANTED

THE WAR
I ALWAYS WANTED

THE ILLUSION OF GLORY AND THE REALITY OF WAR

A SCREAMING EAGLE IN AFGHANISTAN AND IRAQ

BRANDON FRIEDMAN

ZENITH PRESS

First published in 2007 by Zenith Press, an imprint of MBI Publishing Company
LLC, Galtier Plaza, Suite 200, 380 Jackson Street, St. Paul, MN 55101 USA

Zenith Press titles are also available at discounts in bulk quantity for industrial or
sales-promotional use. For details write to Special Sales Manager at MBI Publishing
Company, Galtier Plaza, Suite 200, 380 Jackson Street, St. Paul, MN 55101 USA.

To find out more about our books, join us online at www.zenithpress.com.

Designer: Jennifer Maass
Maps by Phil Schwartzberg, Meridian Mapping

Library of Congress Cataloging-in-Publication Data

Friedman, Brandon, 1978-
   The war I always wanted : the illusion of glory and the reality of war : a Screaming
Eagle in Afghanistan and Iraq / by Brandon Friedman.
      p. cm.
   ISBN-13: 978-0-7603-3150-7 (hardbound w/ jacket) 1. Afghan War, 2001—Personal
narratives, American. 2. Iraq War, 2003—Personal narratives, American. 3. Friedman,
Brandon, 1978- I. Title.
DS371.412.F74 2007
956.7044'3092—dc22
[B]
                              2007012456

Printed in the United States of America

Contents

For Mom, Dad, and Colby,
For Grandpa Brady, an old Marine who
never got to hear these stories,
And for the men of the 1st Battalion, 187th
Infantry Regiment, past and present, who
gave their lives while serving in Iraq

Prologue

First there were mountains. Then there was a desert. And now, sometimes, there are flashbacks. Not full-blown flashbacks, I guess. They're more like super memories—and they creep up on me. Stopped in Dallas traffic *(behind one of the gun trucks)* I glance out of the window of my car and see business people *(Iraqis)* standing on the street corner *(wearing dishdashas)* talking *(waving at me)* on cell phones. My eyes instinctively scan for weapons. Listening to a commercial on the radio, I hear a man's voice *(one of my squad leaders)* selling *("1-6, he's gone down again, over")* new cars. I come home to write, and the chair *(green army cot)* on which I'm sitting makes a familiar creaking noise as I shift *(toss and turn)*, and it reminds me of trying to sleep. Other times it is the craggy earth at nine thousand feet under my worn combat boots. The weight of a Kevlar helmet on my head. The barrels of burning shit. It all sort of blends together.

Sometimes when I look back, I think, "Man, I spent over two years dealing with those fucking wars, and I never saw any *real* combat—not the way I always envisioned it as a kid at least." I never stormed a beach. I never ducked tracer fire while parachuting onto an enemy-held airfield. And my best buddy didn't die in my arms talking about his mom and his girl back home, either. Where I was, everything was so much more *vague* than that.

But I did watch a two-thousand-pound bomb strike the earth less than thirty yards from me and my platoon. In army-speak, that was what we would call a "significant emotional event." And I did shoot some guys—even killed one of them. Not a big deal in the grand scheme of things, but it was a pretty big deal to me. I saw soldiers bending under the stress of guerilla war in mountains and in cities. I met Iraqi translators who walked the thin line between patriotism and treason every day, for months on end. I ate in their homes. I watched their neighbors call them traitors. I could have easily died at least half a dozen times that I know of. I was scared that I was going to die a hundred times that number.

The idea that war changes people is clichéd, but it's true. Going into it, I always thought I'd be above that—immune to it, too well trained for it to affect me, too *professional*. I thought we were beyond all that Vietnam/posttraumatic stress shit. But now I'm in on it.

I have been enlightened.

Now I fear that part of me will always be there—and that that part of me is never coming home. Ever. I'm sure my body will be here, and I'll walk around work or school talking to people, smiling and telling them what it was like and what I'll be doing this weekend and so on. But I'm just not really here.

Instead, I am somewhere else. I'm wearing what has now become old-fashioned desert camouflage. I am thousands of miles from home, in a strange, dusty land where the people speak a language I don't understand. And I am carrying a gun.

I wonder if it will always be this way.

Whoever fights monsters should see to it that in the process he does not become a monster.

—Friedrich Nietzsche

Part I

FEAR

The images of war handed to us, even when they are graphic, leave out the one essential element of war—fear. There is, until the actual moment of confrontation, no cost to imagining glory.

—Chris Hedges, *War Is a Force That Gives Us Meaning*

1

Western Kuwaiti Desert
March 2003

Failure is always an option. People rarely talk about it, but it's always there. It's the giant shrapnel-slinging elephant in the theater of combat that most guys try to put out of their minds. Unfortunately I was never so successful at this, and after I'd been in war for a while, the prospect stressed me out more and more as I went along.

We stood beneath a clear sky in the cream-colored Kuwaiti desert, several miles from what was to become the boundary between sanity and chaos. I was preparing to brief the soldiers I was going to lead across this boundary in the next thirty-six hours. My veteran platoon sergeant, Steve Croom, was next to me. We'd both been in combat before, but neither of us had ever technically invaded a country. Sergeant Croom had been in Iraq in the first Gulf War, but hadn't stayed all that long. I had been to Afghanistan, but in that case I hadn't really invaded anything. I'd more or less just shown up one morning on a transport plane, confused as hell about what the plan was once I walked off the ramp.

Our platoon had been assigned to the 101st Airborne Division's assault command post (ACP). The ACP's commander, a relaxed junior lieutenant colonel named Ahuja, was going to rely on our platoon to get his people three hundred miles inside Iraq during the first two days of the invasion. As far as I knew, there was no plan beyond that.

We had gathered the ACP's officers and senior noncommissioned officers for the briefing. Surrounding us were several dozen yellowish tents that made up the barren outpost known as Camp New Jersey. Several feet away from me was a door flap that made a slapping noise every time a wind gust caught it. In the harsh glare it gave everything a ghost town feel. The already eerie feeling was made even stronger by the way you had to speak up when talking to groups like this. When there was no wind to carry the sound, the sterile land could dull noises, even mute them. It was as if the desert just absorbed them.

Huddled around us, the leaders of the ACP stared intently. They were more bewildered by the whole idea of actually invading a country than we were. The confusion on all sides didn't concern me, however, as the government was paying me a good deal of money to look sharp and act sharp, no matter how confused I actually became. Over the previous year I'd learned that it's best not to try and figure out what *is* happening or what's *going* to happen in combat. This is because *no one knows*. You just have to *go* with it.

I let Sergeant Croom do the talking. As I listened, he touched on how *their* job was to ride in their trucks and sit tight, while *our* job was to do the shooting should it come to that. He said things that all Army sergeants say at one time or another, like, "Stay alert, stay alive," and "Make sure you square each other away." He made no mention of catastrophic failure being an option.

Croom walked with a limp, but it wasn't because of a previous battle injury. He'd been in a car accident a few months before we'd come to Kuwait and had put off the surgery for the war. He'd walked that way from the time I met him, so to me, it made him seem older than he was—which was somewhere in the late thirties.

The only things that made Croom seem true to his age were his two little redheaded girls that he talked about all the time. He had pictures of them dressed as cowgirls for Halloween. When it wasn't them, he was talking about Arkansas. Being from there was a big thing for him. Back home his cell phone voice mail message went something like, "Hey, you've reached Steve . . . I'm prob'ly out in the woods with ma rifle or in my boat catchin' fish right now so if you'll just . . . " and so on. In my mind, he was the guy who got killed in war movies because everyone liked him so much.

As he spoke, trying to make everyone believe that this whole thing was going to go smoothly, the ACP soldiers seemed thankful for the fact that if the road trip into Iraq turned into a two-way rifle range, it would be someone else's problem. They seemed to think that Croom and I had done this before.

An hour later, while we were waiting to move from Camp New Jersey to the attack position closer to the border, the war started with an intrusive blast of sound from the air raid sirens. I am never ready for these things when they happen.

I had left the assembly of vehicles with Sergeant Matt Krueger, one of my section leaders. On the boat ride into the theater, somehow, the flimsy door to the passenger side of my humvee had gone missing. I was determined not to ride into battle without at least the protection of thin vinyl and a soft plastic zippered window. That type of government cost-saving material generally doesn't stop fragmentation from roadside bombs or rocket-propelled grenades, but with me, it was more of a psychological thing. I just wanted a door—any kind of a door.

I had heard that Bravo, my old company, was leaving its only humvee behind because it wouldn't run. Bravo was a rifle company of foot-borne infantry and, theoretically at least, they had no need for trucks. I decided to drive over to the tent section, find it, and cannibalize it by taking one of its doors with me.

So instead of leading my men into battle, banners fluttering and swords valiantly raised, I was wandering around a nearly deserted tent city looking for a vinyl humvee door. And that was when the air raid sirens started wailing. My stomach dropped.

I stretched a chemical protective mask over my head and continued hunting for the door. The mask muffled the scream of the sirens. There was nothing else to do really, except to keep looking. If a missile was going to hit me, it was going to hit me.

I came around a tent and saw the humvee. I walked over to it and carefully removed the door from the hinges and carried it back in the direction of my truck. As I trudged through the sand, kicking it as I went, I gazed at the sky through the hazy plastic lenses of my mask. I was looking for any sign of a descending projectile laced with anthrax or Zyklon-B or whatever. Nothing. Not even a cloud. Just endless blue sky.

When I got back to the truck, Krueger was down on a knee by the bumper. I could see other soldiers doing the same. He looked up at me and told me it had come over the radio that we were supposed to be in a bunker or under the trucks. "Oh," I said. "Hey look, I found a door." Suddenly, the sirens fell silent.

The Voice—that detached presence of authority that guided my life and continually instructed me over my radio—said that an Iraqi al Samoud missile had been fired into Kuwait and that more were expected. The Voice always seemed to come over the airwaves with such disheartening news. I never got the call that I was headed home over the radio. Instead it was always messages like, "Send us two guys for guard duty." Or, "Expect more incoming." Or, "Be prepared to hold that ground."

I took off my mask, walked around to my side of the humvee, and slid the new door into place. Strangely enough, it gave me a warm, safe feeling—as if the door was going to make the whole invasion go well. Then I thought about why that should be, and reasoned that maybe I was losing my mind.

The helplessness you feel when large, explosive objects start falling out of the sky around you is something that's hard to describe. It's a different kind of fear than when you're at least minimally able to defend yourself. This I had learned in the Shah-e-Kot Valley of Afghanistan.

I was around for enough bombing of al Qaeda positions in Afghanistan that once I got home, I got a queasy feeling every time a passenger jet flew overhead. It's the idea of something falling on you, and the idea that it won't reason with you. If it's a person, you can try to understand what he may or may not do in a given situation. If you're outnumbered or outgunned, you can always try to bluff him into thinking that he should mess with someone else. You can't do that with missiles, rockets, and bombs.

As we began to move out from Camp New Jersey, my new door firmly in place, I thought about these things, still so fresh in my memory. I thought about them and I thought about the dreams they induced—of bombs and bullets and people falling all around me. Then I tried to focus on the present. But that never works when memories and dreams of combat are clawing at your addled brain. I kept trying though, and eventually it just made me think about the dreams I'd been having recently. They were dreams of Nikki, the girl who'd stayed with me through the Afghanistan deployment, only to leave me before I came to Kuwait. One night I'd dream she was with another man (which she was), another night I'd dream she was pregnant (which she wasn't), and another night I'd dream she needed my help (which she didn't).

During the buildup for the coming invasion, I'd spent Christmas with Nikki in Dallas, where she was working. All that week she'd made me turn the channel every time there was a story on the massing of troops in Kuwait. The day I left Dallas to return to Fort Campbell, she was a wreck. Her eyes were red-rimmed and she alternated all morning between crying, sniffling, and crying again.

We were in her bedroom and she was sitting cross-legged on the bed. I was standing in front of her, holding my bags in my hands. I was about to leave. She had started crying again. Through the tears, the last thing she said to me was, "I can't do this again."

I guess one war was enough for her.

* * *

As we passed through the gates of Camp New Jersey, never to return, I contemplated that she had at least had the decency to do it between the wars and not right in the middle of one.

Half a mile down the road from New Jersey's front gate, I was ordered over the radio to stop. I was too antsy to sit in the truck, comforted by my new vinyl door, so I got out to stretch my legs. Then, off in the distance and coming from within the camp, I could hear the wail of the air raid sirens again. The Voice over the radio announced an inbound al Samoud missile, this time barreling directly toward us. I just stood there in the bright desert sun beside my truck. This time I didn't bother to even look at the sky. I was a man standing in a drenching downpour without an umbrella, shoulders hunched and dejected-looking. Just standing there and taking it.

And then, with sirens singing in the distance, it hit with a dull *whoomp*. It was far enough away that I didn't see it come in; it was near enough to have gotten my full attention.

The old pang of fear was back. I was being targeted. It is a queasy feeling, unlike anything else, and it comes in waves. Spend enough time in a war and you will become familiar with it. You'll feel it eat slowly at your mind like battery acid, corroding it more and more each day.

Before the wars, I had always been afraid of things like failing a test in school. Or that I'd be late. I was afraid that people at the party would think I looked stupid, or that I'd say something stupid. I was afraid that, when I left the bar, I'd find my car window broken and all my CDs gone.

But fear in war is not like that. This is the type of fear that only comes when you know your life could end at any moment, and you'd never see it coming. This is fear in its purest form.

And it ends up staying with you, too. Because even when the war is over for you, and you're back at home with your family and you no longer fall asleep to the sound of cascading gunfire, that's when you'll notice just how uncomfortable you are when there is seemingly nothing out there in the darkness of which to be afraid.

But in the beginning—a year and half earlier—I knew none of this.

2

Fort Campbell, Kentucky
Fall 2001

"These guys are about to find out the hard way that we ain't the Russians . . . and this ain't Vietnam." My platoon sergeant in Bravo Company, a former army Ranger named Jim Collins, spoke the words deadpan and without emotion. He was always saying things like that.

Earlier that morning we'd been told we were going to war. The World Trade Center was still smoldering and, according to the deployment order I held in my hand, we were part of the payback plan. I had been a platoon leader for fifty-three days.

I was torn. If not for Nikki, the order would have made me happy. I'd spent the last six years like a high school girl waiting to be asked to the prom by the football captain. I'd been waiting for the invitation to the big dance. Now, holding my invitation to the big war in my hand, I couldn't help but think that I'd already gotten Nikki a plane ticket to Fort Campbell for Thanksgiving. And somewhere along the way, that had become more important to me than fighting in a war.

By the time I got to college, I'd fashioned myself into a hawkish war junkie, probably as a means to punish my parents for allowing me to do whatever I wanted as a kid. My mom was an artist and ex-hippie with a rebellious streak; my dad was so passive that I can't ever recall him raising his voice. Our family was middle class and both my brother and I had gone to a private school until we got to high school. We had two dogs and a cat and a big yard in a nice neighborhood. My parents had tried so hard to give us a tranquil, stable home environment. Looking back, I see it backfired for them.

One day in high school I took the Armed Services Vocational Aptitude Battery—the mandatory test they give to juniors. I would have forgotten about it had a recruiter not sent me a postcard telling me that I'd done well. The military scatters thousands of these postcard seeds every year, hoping that just a fraction will catch the eyes of an interested kid and maybe take root—maybe one day sprout into a paratrooper or a fighter pilot. Before I got the postcard, I'd never even thought about joining the Army.

Yet, from the time I was small, I had been attracted to violence, to guns, to *action*. Raised the way I was, these things became the forbidden fruit for a quiet and shy kid who had also liked reading books about animals. And now the recruiter had seized on this one latent passion. He was a pro at it too. What he was selling, I was buying. "They'll teach you to jump out of planes," he'd say. And, "*Sure*, you can still be a sniper if you want to be an officer." Reading the recruiter's postcard had been like the addict's first hit. Going to discuss my options with him in his office was my gateway drug. I walked out with a smile on my face and then went on to study military history in school. I joined the Army. I shaved my head. I voted for Bush in 2000. I learned to shoot. I learned to fight. And I learned to enjoy it.

I stayed like that for five years. I stayed like that until I met Nikki.

It is winter and I'm browsing in the bookstore. She walks past me, heading to a section nearby. I remember her face from high school, back in the mid-1990s. I know she is younger than me. She is beautiful in her black pea coat, blonde hair falling on her shoulders, as she flips through the pages of books in the Career section. In a moment of sheer bravery, I approach her. She is kneeling at one of the shelves. I say something—something that is in all probability ridiculous. She stands up and blushes.

I kissed her for the first time after teaching her to play chess. The first month she stayed at my apartment until late into the night—every night. Suddenly I became more concerned with watching movies at night than with going to the field or qualifying with a new weapon. I started to become self-conscious of all the Army awards and photographs from college that adorned my walls. It all seemed too harsh around her.

Nikki didn't like the Army, and she didn't like that it kept me away from her while she was still in school. Over the span of a few months, her worsening reaction made me start to question whether or not *I* still liked the Army. My loyalties became conflicted. I couldn't explain why, but a green-eyed girl in Louisiana was quickly deconstructing a fanaticism that had taken years to cultivate and mature.

Without a word I could see that she saw herself in a competition with the Army. It made me see for the first time that I had become hooked on the narcotic intensity of destructive weapons and the sheer power of human will and determination. I was obsessed with how these things could be meshed into the ultimate war hammer for the forces of good. This is what the Army taught, and this is what I, the student, wanted to hear.

But Nikki made me realize that I hadn't been raised that way, that somewhere inside I knew that this was no way to live life. With such a mentality, I would burn out sooner rather than later. I knew on some level that I was rebelling from what I thought people expected me to do. I began to think that somehow, perhaps, I should consider extricating myself from the lifestyle. Maybe become normal—start a family, get an office job. Sleep under a roof, not trees.

This personal coming-of-age crisis couldn't have come at a worse time either. It peaked roughly two weeks before everything changed late in the summer of 2001.

I really can't recall what the battalion commander said as we stood in formation that morning, other than the fact that it involved me and an airplane, some guns, and at least one third-world country. I did manage to recognize that my parents' worst nightmare was unfolding in front of me. But rather than being energized by the prospect of hunting down Osama bin Laden and his minions, I felt deflated about having to break the news to Nikki.

I'd been waiting for this moment for six years. I had finally been chosen as one of the few to represent the United States in a war of vengeance, and now, at what could have been my supreme moment, I was hesitant.

Until recently, the idea of sacrifice had never entered my mind, even as I'd entered the Army. Being a soldier had always been such a good time that I never considered it a sacrifice in any way. Sacrifice was always such a theoretical and distant ideal. But this was something new—something tangible. I was going to *lose* the chance to be with Nikki, and that was something of which I felt desperately in need.

The deployment order wasn't much of a surprise. My unit—the 1st Battalion of the 187th Infantry Regiment (the 3rd Brigade) of the 101st Airborne Division—had been in every major conflict since World War II. It was there, in Japan, that the unit had gotten its nickname. From that point on, the soldiers of the unit were called Rakkasans—Rakkasan being the Japanese word meaning "falling down umbrella." It was a reference to the parachutes they used in World War II. Why the Japanese had a word for "falling down umbrella" but not for "parachute" was a question often asked in our unit.

After our morning formation I headed upstairs to my office. It was basically a small closet that I shared with my platoon sergeant, Jim Collins. In it were two desks, a wall locker, and two chairs. In contrast to other offices, ours was relatively bare. Most offices had framed photographs of soldiers, posters, awards, and certificates on the walls. Ours simply had two dry erase boards and one small bulletin board.

I found Sergeant Collins standing, facing the bulletin board, looking at a note he had stuck up there earlier. Without turning around, he said quietly, "Looks like we're headed down range to lay some waste." I took my seat and started fiddling through some stuff in my desk, looking for the instruction manual on "How to Deploy a Rifle Platoon Halfway Around the World." Sergeant Collins sat down and we started hashing out a plan. A few minutes later the conversation turned to history and philosophy. We talked about al Qaeda, we talked about the Taliban, and we talked about the Russians in Afghanistan and the United States in Vietnam. Before we left the office to brief the squad leaders, Collins looked me in the eye and said, "These guys are about to find out the hard way that we ain't the Russians . . . and this ain't Vietnam."

As we walked out, I realized that I was jealous of his enthusiasm.

Collins was known throughout the infantry and special operations communities as "Jimbo" or "Jungle Jim." I commanded Bravo Company's 1st Platoon to the extent that a green second lieutenant is capable, but if I was Luke Skywalker, Collins was Obi Wan. Collins had served for ten years in the special operations community before leaving to take control of his first platoon in the 101st Airborne. He was about six feet tall, lean and cut. When it came to exercise, he equated moderation with eating greasy cheeseburgers: they were both dangerously bad for you. For Collins, a morning jog was not complete unless he had tried to "pop" his heart. We would lift weights and I would end up standing aside breathlessly as he completed a chest workout of fifteen sets to failure on the bench press.

Collins would say things like, "I wanna jam my bayonet between a guy's ribs and watch his life blood run out." Or, after choking out some other sergeant in a round of hand-to-hand combat, he'd stand up, dust himself off, and say in a low, slow, and drawn-out Clint Eastwood-as-Dirty Harry-voice, "A man's got to know his limitations." People who didn't know him well always laughed uncomfortably at the proclamations. But the guys liked it. The ironic thing was that, before the wars, we had always thought he was *joking*.

* * *

For a week we waited for a plane to come and take us away, each day thinking that that would be the day. During that time Collins did his best to keep everyone's minds occupied. We would practice hand and arm signals and covering each other in the open. We practiced working with our radios and we assembled and disassembled our weapons against the clock hundreds of times. When that got old, we did *combatives*.

"Combatives" was army-speak for hand-to-hand combat—something that I liked, but he loved. He was so into combatives that he would walk around the battalion, the post exchange, or the mall, with it on his mind. He would pick out some unassuming guy walking the other way (usually a big guy), and he'd lean over to me and say, "See that guy? I wanna fight him just to see where I stand."

Specialist James Taylor, my radioman, was standing next to me one afternoon when Collins suggested it. "Aw come on, Sergeant Collins . . . do we have to do that shit again?" the radio-telephone operator pleaded.

"Shut yer yap, Taylor," came the response. "You don't have a choice."

It became a full-blown company tournament on the lawn outside the battalion headquarters building. Collins couldn't have been more in his element—men were fighting, locked in matches of physical skill and endurance, testing each other's limits. It was an exercise in yelling, spittle, dust, and sweat. Even Collins, who was only refereeing, had a wild look in his eyes. If we had only had chainsaws and a giant fence on which to climb, it would have been like Thunderdome—with Sergeant Collins playing the part of Tina Turner. I could hear the chanting in my head: *Two men enter, one man leaves! Two men enter, one man leaves!*

As the organizer, Collins paired me with 2nd Platoon's leader, Sam Edwards. Sam was the senior platoon leader in the battalion, and he had a reputation for being one of the most competent, yet unassuming officers in the unit. He was married to his college sweetheart and, according to Sam, she was the only reason he'd made it through school. They had a baby girl who was several months old. I personally thought he was a great guy and I still do. However, none of these facts stopped me from trying to choke him nearly unconscious that afternoon in Collins' submission match.

The final call came at six o'clock on a Sunday morning. Shortly after I arrived on post, about 150 of us filed into the Mann Theater on Fort Campbell for our mission briefing. Sitting in the theater and watching a Powerpoint slideshow, I learned that the mission was taking us to a place called Jacobabad in the Indus River Valley of Pakistan. Adjacent to the city was a Pakistani Air Force Base that was being used by a range of U.S. special operations forces, as well as by a handful of secretive U.S. government organizations.

Our mission, as it stood, was to relieve a group of Marines already there, in order to protect the base from terrorist attacks as U.S. forces operated from within. Any follow-on missions or action we might see in Afghanistan, we were told, would come about once we were in country. For now, they said, just secure the airfield.

The disappointment was palpable and could be read on the face of every soldier in the theater—in their slumped shoulders and their dejected exhalations. Our secret day-dreamy visions of landing on a hostile runway, offloading, and gloriously seizing an airfield were decimated for the time being. It seemed that we were going to fly halfway around the world just to sit around in Pakistan. Nobody wanted to die in a bloody firefight, but nobody wanted to spend time guarding an airfield either. It's the soldier's paradox.

I didn't want to leave Nikki, but I still had enough fervor left inside that allowed me to ride the wave of testosterone that permeated the building. Having been resigned to a long separation, I told myself that it would at least be for a good cause. Might as well make the most of it, I had thought.

With that attitude, we lifted off the ground that morning in an air force C-17 and headed into the unknown. We carried only ourselves, our weapons, and our memories—memories of easier, peaceful times with friends and family.

3

Jacobabad, Pakistan
Winter 2002

Sergeant Collins is walking awkwardly with his rifle in his left hand—something I think odd until I see his right arm. He has it crooked slightly at the elbow and I can see dark red blood running down his arm and dripping off his hand as he walks. I can't tell if the blood is coming from his arm or his side. He is looking straight ahead as he walks. His face conveys a mixture of fear and confusion, pain and determination—as if he wants to keep moving despite his injury. He then turns and looks me in the eye. "I can't find a medic," he says.

That's when I awoke. I looked over at Collins' cot next to mine. He was snoring softly, curled up in the fetal position and still wearing his boots. The blood was only in my head. After four months of wasting away in Pakistan, wrestling weekly with the constant stress of false alarms, the environment was starting to get to me.

Thanksgiving, Christmas, and New Year's were behind us. Then February 2002 had come and gone, leaving us still closer to Bombay than Kabul. While the special ops guys handled the war in Afghanistan, our days were spent defending the perimeter of a smoggy airfield. The routine was mind-numbing, the boredom nearly unbearable. Most days the guys in my platoon spent eight hours manning bunkers on the edge of the airfield. They were supposed to be on the lookout for any signs of misplaced extremism, but their disenchantment showed through. After a few months each bunker had an infantryman's Sistine Chapel-like quality to it. I'd stick my head in and read the ceilings and walls. "I hate the Army." "Soldier A is a fudgepacker." "Soldier B can suck my nuts." "Elected leader C is a moron and hypocrite." Often, detailed drawings accompanied the claims.

We spent four months watching it not rain. Planes would land, planes would take off. Other planes would land, other planes would take off. Like all the people back home, we were watching the war play out on TV. I knew we weren't going to Afghanistan. Despite all the buildup, we'd been relegated to an uninteresting support mission—a long, drawn-out anticlimax with a smattering of false alarms.

As events unfolded around me at the beginning of March 2002, I knew something wasn't right. It had started as just a trickle of disconcerting information. But by that afternoon it had become a torrent of bad news. One soldier was reported killed, several wounded. Vehicles were being abandoned, and the Americans were in retreat. As reports streamed from the television, shock began setting in.

At the time, only one American soldier had been killed at the hands of an armed enemy in nearly a decade. To most of the guys in the unit, the idea of someone *really* dying in combat was still abstract. We had been rocked gently to sleep every night by the thought that we would never be sent into a situation that wasn't peacekeeping, security, or just something totally lopsided. A battle this size hadn't happened since Vietnam.

Operation Anaconda was a legendary battle two days after it started. By the time it ended, it was already gaining an odd sort of mythical status in Army circles. Even though it was a small operation when compared to everything that happened later in Iraq, the mystique of Anaconda has remained.

It had all the elements of a memorable battle, I guess. Elite American units. An enemy willing to stand his ground. Sweeping landscapes. American troops pinned down. Army Rangers refusing to leave a man behind. Massive bombing. Snipers. Mortars. And most of all, payback for September 11.

It sounded great. It was everything I'd ever wanted as a kid.

The operation was named Anaconda because it was designed to put the squeeze on hundreds al Qaeda fighters found massing in the Shah-e-Kot Valley of eastern Afghanistan. Aiming to capture or kill them all in one place, the Army had devised a plan to encircle the valley with elements of the 101st Airborne and 10th Mountain Divisions. Once the terrorists were trapped, friendly Afghan forces and their U.S. Army Special Forces sponsors would attack into the valley, covered by close air support.

I gazed at the TV screen standing next to Sergeant Collins. Things just didn't sound right. *Abandoning vehicles?* After spending several minutes scrutinizing every word out of the mouth of the newscaster, I began to think that if something had gone so terribly wrong, then it wouldn't stand for long.

Surely someone would be sent in quickly to rectify the situation. Suddenly a thought scrolled across the ticker in my brain. This was an *important* thought. *Someone would be sent . . . .*

I hurried with Sergeant Collins to the TOC. Inside it were computer terminals from which we could email. I quickly tapped out letters to Nikki and my parents. I told them that something was happening and to just watch the news. I didn't know anything else.

We walked back outside, almost bumping into another company's commander. When he recognized us, he stopped and asked if we'd heard the news yet. I said, "No, what?"

"Your streak of days with nothing to do but lift weights and jerk off," he said, "is over."

It turned out that the 101st and 10th Mountain soldiers had been inserted into the mountains below al Qaeda positions, allowing the defenders to fire on them from above. Then it had gotten worse when an air force AC-130 shot up the main column of attacking Afghans and Green Berets, causing the Afghans to quit the fight.

Only then, with the operation unraveling, did we get the call in Jacobabad.

We received AT4s, claymore mines, and hand grenades. When I was handed my grenades, it occurred to me that I hadn't held one since I'd been in infantry school nine months earlier.

I held the first one up, inspecting the pin and the spoon. The steel sphere was cold in the night air and, as usual, heavier than it looked. It reminded me of a bloated egg sac, mature and ready to burst at any second. I tore off a piece of tape and wrapped it around the pin and spoon of the grenade. There was no point in taking chances. Accidentally getting one stuck on some equipment and having it explode on the airplane would have made for a less-than-optimal start. The guys with claymores went diligently through the carrying cases in which they came, checking to make sure each one had the mine, the wire, the clacker, and the test kit. While I was tying down all my equipment inside my ruck, I listened to the din of voices in the night air. I heard somebody laughing. Then, over the sounds of packing and anxious conversation, I heard Collins' voice: "They shouldn't have told *me* that in basic training," he said, "because *I* have a gun. And I *will* travel." There was some more laughing. They were cheerful at least.

After the weapons had been issued, guys started putting together packages of stuff to mail home. It was everything you wanted to keep, but didn't have room for in Afghanistan. I threw one together that consisted of an old MRE box filled with all the mail I'd received, a letter to my parents, and some books I'd read. I gave the box to a soldier we were leaving behind along with a twenty-dollar bill and told him to keep the change.

I lay shivering on my cot late that night, staring up at the ceiling of the hardened aircraft hangar in which we lived. I had no idea who we were really going after in Afghanistan. Thus far they were only being vaguely described as "terrorists." I did know, however, that if these were the same people who had helped launch the September 11 attacks, they were serious about their business. Because those people, whoever they were—their hatred had been pure. That much I knew. I had tried to dismiss them as insane, but in the end, couldn't talk myself into it. And that was the disturbing part. They weren't insane. Insane people couldn't have pulled off an operation like that. These were intelligent, reasoning beings so consumed by the most crystallized strain of hatred that they were willing to kill themselves along with other men, women, children, Muslims and non-Muslims whom they'd never met. I contemplated what would make a person become like that. And if this was indeed the same group of people, I wondered how they would react to those who weren't unarmed airline passengers or unsuspecting high-rise office workers. I wondered how deep this hatred went.

For the second time in four months we were headed for the unknown. My mind drifted to something I'd heard one of my soldiers say earlier in the day: "What's that, Lassie? The Rakkasans are coming?" As I lay there on the creaking cot, I imagined a cave. *Inside are two terrorists. One is wearing a turban; the other wears a field jacket and carries a radio in his right hand. They are talking to each other. All of a sudden Lassie walks in the entrance of the cave and stops in front of them. They stop talking. Lassie barks . . . twice. The terrorists look at each other and say something in Arabic. I see subtitles in English. They say, "What's that, Lassie? The Rakkasans are coming?"* Under the cover of my thin poncho, I finally fell asleep.

There are only a few windows on a C-130, and even those are just small holes in the fuselage about eight inches in diameter. There was one near me and, if I craned my neck just the right way, I could see out. Through this tiny porthole I was able to view the vast stretches of Pakistan's western desert. Almost immediately after takeoff, the surface of the earth below us began to crinkle and rise up, in ridge after ridge of rugged mountains. It was not only a spectacle of enormousness, but also one of uninhabitable desolation for as far as the eye could see. There were no roads; there were no buildings; there was nothing to suggest people had even *been* to this part of the world. For nearly two hours I stared down, mesmerized, at the alien landscape. At some point, as we flew north over this seemingly boundless stretch of wasteland, we crossed into Afghanistan.

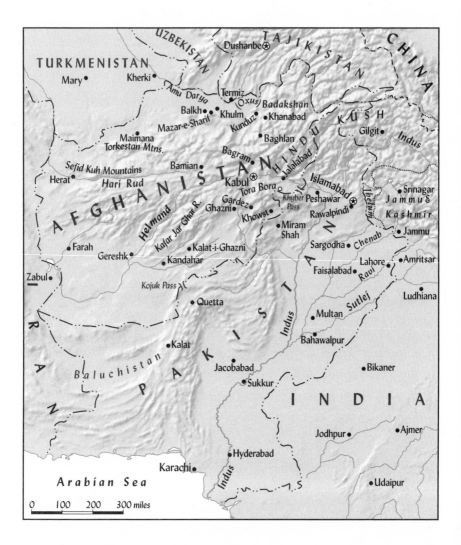

TURKMENISTAN

UZBEKISTAN

TAJIKISTAN

CHINA

Mary

Kherki

Dushanbe ⊗

Amu Darya

Termiz

(Oxus)

Balkh

Khulm

Badakshan

Mazar-e-Sharif

Kunduz

Khanabad

Maimana

Torkestan Mtns.

Baghlan

HINDU

KUSH

Gilgit

Indus

Sefid Kuh Mountains

Bamian

Bagram

Herat

Hari Rud

Kabul ⊗

Jalalabad

AFGHANISTAN

Tora Bora

Islamabad ⊗

Srinagar

Gardez

Khyber

Pass

Peshawar

Jammu &

Ghazni

Khowst

Rawalpindi

Kashmir

Helmand

Kafar Jar Ghar R.

Miram

Shah

Jammu

Farah

Kalat-i-Ghazni

Sargodha

Chenab

Gereshk

Kandahar

Faisalabad

Lahore

Amritsar

Zabul

Ravi

Kojuk Pass

Ludhiana

Quetta

PAKISTAN

Sutlej

Indus

Multan

Kalat

Bahawalpur

Baluchistan

Jacobabad

Bikaner

IRAN

Sukkur

INDIA

Jodhpur

Ajmer

Hyderabad

Karachi

Indus

Udaipur

Arabian Sea

0   100   200   300 miles

4

Bagram, Afghanistan
March 2002

My first thought was: *Those can't be real.*

Some several hundred million years ago, the Indian sub-continent started its slow geologic crash into Asia. The wreckage is spectacular—an arc of torn, folded, and cantilevered stone that roughly tracks the border of northern India and Pakistan. Its eastern leg is the higher and better-known Himalayan Range, stretching across India, Nepal, and China. The western leg, which reaches across India, Pakistan, and Afghanistan, is known as the Hindu Kush.

In the middle is a small town on the Shomali Plain with a long, Soviet-built runway. Fought over by the Russians and the mujahideen, the Tajiks, the Taliban, and the Americans, the battle-scarred town is surrounded on three sides by these geologic cathedrals that rise nearly twenty thousand feet.

The first thing I was told when I stepped off the plane in Bagram was, "Don't step off the concrete. Mines everywhere."

A generation of fighting in and around the airfield had left it littered with every conceivable kind of unexploded ordnance. Wandering the demined areas, I found myself in a warped Wild West. Tents bristling with antennae had cropped up amidst shattered mud-brick buildings, and bearded Special Forces soldiers with laser range finders and satellite phones milled about with Afghans who had drifted off the pages of a nineteenth-century storybook.

I was standing beside my ruck when a good friend of mine on the battalion staff approached me. I could tell by the look on his face that things weren't going well.

He had been watching live footage of the battle, beamed directly from a Predator drone. He told me that seven hours earlier a combination of army rangers and Navy SEALs had attempted to insert a team onto the mountain that dominated the eastern side of the Shah-e-Kot Valley. The Afghan name for the twelve-thousand-foot peak was Takhur Gar; the U.S. Army had dubbed it Objective Ginger. They had gone in to establish an observation post on the high ground in order to regain flagging momentum. Just like the 101st and 10th Mountain before them, they landed in a hornet's nest of al Qaeda fighters. A Navy SEAL fell out of his helicopter and they were trying to get him back. We didn't know that he had already been executed.

"Do you know how lucky you are to be able to lead an infantry platoon into a fight like this?" my friend asked. "I would trade places with you in a heartbeat." He was trying to be upbeat about the whole thing.

Lucky is when you win the lottery. This was not lucky. I knew he was trying to help, but for the first time, I was starting to stress. So I just said with a wry smile, "Speak for yourself, dude." What I wanted to say was, "You're not going in. It looks different from this angle."

I left Sergeant Collins with the platoon and began to meander about with Sam Edwards and our boss, Captain Rob K. All we knew was that a battle to which we had been invited was raging, and we were late. Walking aimlessly among tents and buildings, we came to the realization that everyone with information was either on a radio, glued to a television screen, or fighting in the valley itself. Eventually we stumbled into a green tent with a sign outside that said in block letters: SECRET. Inside, we found a scale model of the operational area.

The sand table (as they're called) displayed two prominent ridges on either side of a wide valley. The western ridge, the smaller of the two, was marked "The Whale;" the valley, "Shah-e-Kot." The eastern ridge had placards on a number of spots. Each label was a separate objective area, and they all had women's names. I knew of "Ginger," the looming anchor of the eastern ridge, but now, as I scanned the model from north to south, I saw "Amy," "Betty," "Cindy," Diane," "Eve," and "Heather."

Captain K. thrust at Sam and me two crappy, photo-copied maps he'd received from somebody. He also gave us each a transparent overlay and told us to start copying the objectives from a large map hung on the wall of the tent. Another glance at the map I held in my hand, and I knew it was a waste of time. It was unreadable and using it wouldn't have made any sense at all. But Captain K., who had only assumed command of Bravo Company a month earlier, was intent on going through the motions.

Now, upon being commissioned as an officer all the way through my army schooling, I always had this irrational fear of being shot in the back in combat by one of my own guys. It shaped the way I tried to lead. I always took the attitude that my men didn't work for me, but that I worked for them. My *job* was to provide for *them*, to make sure they received proper training; that they had the right equipment; that they knew what to do in a firefight; that they had good food to eat; that they were safe; that they could call home; that their families were taken care of. I reasoned that if I concentrated on those things, they would take care of the hard stuff—closing with and destroying the enemy, thereby allowing all of us to go home in one piece.

I tried not to be the guy who thinks he's smarter than his men just because he went to college. Or the boor who gets off on being "in charge." Or the glory hunter who thinks his men exist for the sole purpose of helping him to propel his career. I thought it was more important to impress the guys below me than those above me. Hearing my commander say, "Friedman is a good officer who really keeps his men in line," is nice. But I would much prefer to overhear one of my privates say, "You know, Lieutenant Friedman sure is goofy, but I'd follow him anywhere. You know *he'd* take care of us."

That idea of being scorned by forty dedicated infantrymen kept me awake at night. This, however, was not something that seemed to concern our new commander.

Captain K. was a big, serious-looking guy with a permanent scowl on his face. He accused me in his office once of being "too happy-go-lucky." Captain K. was long on infantry tactics, but short on people skills. And he always excused his inability to communicate with others by calling it "tough love." The way I saw it, his tough love was based out of the insecurity that people wouldn't think he was tough *enough*. Whereas most soldiers kept pictures of their wives and girlfriends inside their helmets, the single Captain K. kept his dog's collar in a zip lock bag. More commando than ladies' man, I guess he thought that affection for a carnivorous animal, bred for hunting with fangs and claws, would dissuade anyone from questioning why he was single.

Once, after eye surgery (the irritatingly painful photore-fractive keratectomy, or PRK), I was eating breakfast across the table from him at the chow hall on Fort Campbell. The doctor had ordered me not to run or work out for my first full week back at work after the surgery. My medical profile stated that the most I could do was to "walk at own pace and distance." Still doped up on Percocet, that was about all I could manage anyway. Over scrambled eggs, Captain K. asked me what I'd done for PT that morning. Since we usually scoffed at such medical profiles, especially those with the kinds of instructions I'd received, I responded, half-jokingly, that I'd walked at my own pace and distance. Captain K. had authorized the surgery, so I assumed he'd get it.

Instead, he stopped eating and looked at me, suddenly enraged that I would be so weak as to follow the medical doctor's directions. "I'll throw you out of that window," he said with the point of a fork, "at my own pace and distance. Don't you ever say something like that again, Friedman." He never liked to call his subordinates, especially NCOs, by their proper rank either—it was always just the last name. Everyone at the table around us, including a few other commanders, stopped chewing and became quiet. They were trying to discern whether or not he was serious. I knew he was, however, as I had gotten used to dealing with those types of remarks. I knew that Captain K. was embarrassed that one of his platoon leaders had revealed what he perceived to be a weakness in front of the other commanders.

I just said, "Okay. All right. I'm done here." And I took my tray and walked out.

I never understood why he was like that.

No sooner had we started copying onto the maps, than another staff officer burst through the door of the tent. He was out of breath and said he'd been looking for us. Captain K. asked him what was going on and this is what he said: Some shit is fucked up. Some other shit is confused. And there's still some other shit we don't know about. His mission: Get us into the shit as quickly as possible. When would that be? Shit . . . either today, tonight, or tomorrow. No one really knew.

As the sun began to drop behind the mountains, the temperature began to plummet. What had been a pleasant, cloudless day with a temperature in the low sixties, was turning into a bitterly cold, miserable night. Just before sunset, Sergeant Collins and I located the tent that belonged to our platoon for the night. There was nothing inside but hard-packed dirt. I picked out a nice spot of soil in between Sergeant Collins and my RTO, Specialist Taylor. Taylor and I grabbed our ponchos, reckoning that a poncho, a tent, and body heat would be enough to sustain us through the night. Sergeant Collins grabbed what looked like an old, muddy, piece of olive drab canvas he had found. I was spreading my poncho on the floor when Taylor stopped what he was doing and looked at Sergeant Collins.

"That's disgusting. You're gonna sleep under that?" he asked.

"Shut yer ballwasher, Taylor" came the response. "We'll see who stays warm tonight."

As dawn crept over the peaks ten hours later, I wished I had had an old, rotten piece of canvas with which to sleep. Those ten interminable hours had been my first experience with the northern Afghan night. The cold had penetrated the defenses of the thin tent almost immediately after the sun's retreat, and only slightly later it penetrated the defenses of my even thinner poncho. I had lain awake all night, teeth chattering, trying to find the "warm position," a mythical arrangement of body parts that desperately cold people mistakenly think can save them. During all the tossing and turning, I had listened in the darkness to helicopters returning. In their bellies were the dead and wounded from the day's battle.

It was a beautiful day—not too cold and not too hot. Miles away, wisps of snow blew off of the higher peaks to the north, against a royal blue sky. At midmorning we began a long walk out to an improvised firing range to resight our weapons. It was located at the northern end of the runway, about a mile from the tent area. Along the way I had plenty to think about. It was now eight dead. Fifty wounded. In my mind, this would have been unthinkable a week earlier. Not since the fight in Mogadishu in October of 1993 had anything like this happened.

I was disappointed and concerned, but not yet terrified. I was disappointed on the count that I had naively envisioned being a hero, as too many American kids do. I had seen myself swooping in to save the day in a terribly important battle. Now, as an adult being force-fed a reality sandwich, it looked like I was going to be the underdog. And the concern—well, it looked like we could end up fighting for our lives.

We marched in silence, each soldier alone with his thoughts. In the distance I could make out the Apaches that had returned from the previous day's fight. From what I had heard, all six birds had received fire, and several had been critically disabled. A few of the pilots had been wounded, some seriously. I couldn't imagine Apaches—bristling with rocket pods, missiles, and machine guns—being shot up.

As we approached the tarmac where the attack helicopters were parked, I could see that something just didn't *look* right. Angles were wrong. The helicopters themselves *looked* wrong. From a hundred yards away I could see this. Coming from Fort Campbell, I'd seen Apaches every day, and these just didn't look *right*. As we got closer, I could see what it was. They looked *small*.

They looked broken. They looked beaten down and exhausted. I still don't understand how an inanimate object could be perceived and personified in such a way, but that is the only way I can describe it. They looked *physically smaller* than I remembered them being. Maybe that was my imagination. However, when I got within a few feet of them, what I saw was not my imagination.

The helicopters had been thrashed by the al Qaeda fighters. Each had flown through a withering barrage of gunfire, receiving multiple hits from tail to nose. The first thing I noticed was the copious amount of hydraulic fluid on the first bird. It had been sprayed all over the tail section of the aircraft. I looked closer and could see large bullet holes in a connect-the-dots pattern along the side as well. They looked to be the size of those fired from AK-47s.

The second looked worse. Along with numerous holes of varying sizes, its windshield had been shattered, parts of it broken out completely. Along the side of the aircraft were other bits and pieces of broken off or jagged pieces hanging from the fuselage. From behind me I could hear the muffled sounds of, "*Shiiiit,*" and "*ahh Christ,*" and "*mother . . . fucker,*" coming from the platoon. Having now seen the Apaches up close, I was no longer disappointed and concerned. Now I was terrified. Keeping my thoughts to myself, I continued walking toward the range with the guys, just taking it all in.

"Ahhhh, shit!"

The crack of the first volley at the range was followed instantaneously by a louder pop. I looked over my left shoulder. It was Private First Class Bumstead, from 3rd Platoon. He hadn't screamed it—he'd just announced it like he'd dropped a bag of groceries. As I stared at him, I could see blood starting to soak into his torn uniform just above one of his knees. Instinctively, I walked toward him, as did others. Immediately two guys grabbed him and lowered him to the ground. It was then that the pain hit him. He started wiggling his legs. "*Sssssss . . . mother . . . fucker . . . shitshitshitshitshit!*" He was trying to stifle it.

A minute earlier, the gunners and ammo bearers had ambled over to the firing line and kneeled down. They had brushed away the old, spent shell casings left behind by other units. They had assumed the prone position, taking aim behind their weapons. Then one of them had shot a land mine.

My medic ran to Bumstead's side and began assessing the damage. A piece of shrapnel had sliced into Bumstead's thigh, narrowly missing an artery. Two other soldiers in 3rd Platoon were hit as well—both in the hands. As Doc worked, Captain K. called off the range.

So that's what blood looks like coming out of soldiers. I can deal with this. I heard the first sergeant call my name. I answered him, "Sir?"

Sir? Where did that come from? Why am I calling him sir? "I, uh, wh . . . what, First Sergeant?"

He looked at me inquisitively. I had just called him sir, and I could see his wheels turning. After hearing it, he was wondering the same thing I was. *Will Friedman be able to keep his shit together in front of his guys.* "Lieutenant Friedman, is your platoon ready to go?"

"Uh, yeah . . . yeah, we're ready to go."

"Okay," he said, "get Sergeant Collins and you guys can head back." As I turned, I could feel him watching me.

If I thought I'd had a lot to think about on the way to the range, it had increased exponentially in the intervening period. For starters, I knew I was going to die. For a cocky, arrogant Rakkasan with years of specialized training, this was not something I had ever expected to feel in combat. Prior to the last forty-eight hours, I had fully expected the enemy to cringe and grovel before us, the vaunted 101st Airborne Division. It had become such a rarity to see an enemy of the United States stand their ground in a pitched battle. And now eight special operations troops, including four army Rangers, were dead. The 101st and 10th Mountain had over fifty wounded. All of the Apaches were down. And now it was *my* turn to take a whack at the situation.

The hero goggles were now completely off. As Celine's tormented character says in his novel *Journey to the End of the Night*, "I had grown phobically allergic to heroism . . . I was cured. Radically cured." The medicine had worked instantaneously. At that moment, for the first time in my life, I sincerely wanted an office job. In my head I could see the bullet holes that had peppered the Apaches—except now they formed words along the fuselage that said, "Get the fuck out of here." If someone had offered me the chance to buy my way out at that point, I would have given away all my money and everything I owned. I probably would have given away much more than that.

I saw clearly all the things I was never going to do. I thought about Nikki. I thought about how I would never get the chance to marry her. I would never have kids and get to watch them grow up. There were so many things I'd wanted to do. I was going to take flying lessons. I wanted to backpack across Europe. Now it had all been ruined. This was it. I realized that my parents would bury their oldest son. I knew that I wouldn't get the chance to tell them goodbye. How would they get notified? Who would call Nikki? How would my brother handle it? *Goddammit.*

Stop.

Focus.

Desperate to carry more bullets, mortar rounds, and water, we started tossing everything we didn't need. We ditched our hygiene kits, we ditched most of our cold weather gear, and we didn't even take ponchos to build little shelters against the snow. Even so, as a platoon leader with a lighter than average set of equipment, mine weighed over a hundred pounds.

As we stood out in the sun trying in vain to lighten our loads, Bumstead and the other two returned. They had been stitched up and given a clear bill of health by the medics. Bumstead carried shrapnel in his leg and a bottle of pain pills. After being offered the opportunity to stay behind due to his injury, he politely declined and said he would rather go in with his platoon. There wasn't even any hesitation, really. I had to respect that. I'm not sure what I would've done if someone had offered me the same deal.

I still respected Bumstead for what he did that day even after he went AWOL before we left for Iraq. I didn't really know him well, but when I heard about it, I figured he probably hadn't wanted to test his luck again. Maybe between Afghanistan and Iraq, the shrapnel worked its way from his leg and into his head. Like Nikki, I guess maybe one war was enough for him, too.

We couldn't get everyone on the first lift that afternoon, but another bird was going to be available twelve hours later. *Okay. So how many guys can we take on the first lift?* Ninety. Forty-five per bird. *Has this ever been done on a Chinook before?* Probably not. *What if the landing zone is hot?* You've seen *Saving Private Ryan*, right?

I had nobody to blame for this except myself. Too many fucking movies as a kid; as a teenager; as an adult.

The plan materialized slowly, emerging piece by piece from the fog. We were to set down on a landing zone somewhere on Objective Amy, the northernmost area in the operation. The company was to establish a "blocking position" in order to prevent the escape of fleeing al Qaeda fighters. The fact that we were being sent to "block" and not to "attack" worked a bit to allay my cranky mood at having to die by early evening. It was much harder to get you or your men killed in a blocking position than in an all-out assault up a hill.

But then, as if on cue, I was warned by someone that every single LZ in the operation had been "hot" so far. A "hot" LZ is one in which you're getting shot at as you're coming off the bird. On D-Day in 1944, Omaha Beach would have been aptly described as "hot." *Is our LZ gonna be hot?* Nobody knew.

Loading a helicopter for an air assault mission, you can't hear anything and nobody understands each other's hand gestures. And it's terribly windy under the blades. Packing forty-five combat-laden troops into the rear of the aircraft is like a cross between musical chairs and Twister. Guys get on; guys get settled; then we wouldn't have enough room. So guys would get off; guys would get on again; guys would get settled; then we'd do it over again. For twenty minutes we made such feeble attempts. Captain K. had wanted to be the last guy on the bird so that he could be the first guy out the door when we landed. He wanted to be a hero. It was fine by me, but Sergeant Collins and Sergeant Tom Dougherty, my 1st Squad leader, talked him out of it.

Finally settled and earplugged inside the rumbling bird, I had just started to envision what a hot LZ was going to look like in the mountains, when someone started pushing me from behind. I looked back. He pointed to the rear of the bird. Standing on the ramp, ten soldiers between us, was our executive officer. His helmet had gone sideways, his eyes were blazing, and he was screaming something. I couldn't hear anything, but I could read his lips yelling, "Friedman!!!" Based on the emotional expression on his face and the fact that I hadn't been able to hear anything, I determined that he had probably been yelling my name for a while now. I said, "What?"

"Fuckin' c'mere, goddammit!"

So again, everybody in front had to offload.

Captain K., Sam Edwards, and 3rd Platoon's acting platoon leader, were already gathered around a John Deere Gator. On the Gator was the air liaison. With him, he brought the new mission. Now we were to land at Objective Amy. Then we were to "attack" south to some random grid coordinate he gave us. If we weren't involved in heavy fighting, we were to establish an LZ for the last Chinook. It would be arriving around 4 a.m. the next morning, in about twelve hours. I was placing my notes back in my cargo pocket when, over the roar of the engines, Sam tapped me on the shoulder and yelled, "Hey man . . . the fun meter . . . It's pegged!" He smiled sarcastically, shaking his head and then turning away.

I got back on the bird. All of 1st Platoon's eyes were on me. *How the fuck do you give an operations order on a moving Chinook?* A formal operations order is usually several pages worth of detailed instructions, but that wasn't happening. I took out my notebook and tore off four little strips of paper. I scribbled some words on them, and then, since I was toward the middle, passed them in the direction of each corner of the aircraft. It only vaguely resembled a plan, but it was *something*. It looked like this:

NEW PLAN:
Get off bird.
Go left.
Attack.
Grid: MN 27189533

It wasn't quite the way I'd learned to compose written orders in Army schools, but this was all the guys were gonna get. I figured if we got lit up as soon as we touched down, it wouldn't matter anyhow.

Suddenly the intensity of the bird's vibrations picked up. It lurched forward and I could feel the ground leave us. The bird began to pick up speed and we headed south, toward the Shah-e-Kot Valley and Objective Amy.

The two Chinooks flew in attack formation, one behind the other, not more than fifty or sixty feet off the ground. As I looked out the rear door, beyond the tail gunner, I could see the second bird fifty or sixty yards behind us. Skimming above the ground, I could see a trail of swirling dust it was leaving in its wake. I looked through the porthole windows and stared across the fast-moving Shomali Plain. On both sides, mountains stood ominously. I felt like they were waiting for us.

We had been in the air for about twenty minutes when out of the blue the door gunners on either side of the aircraft cut loose with long bursts from their machine guns. My head jerked up, my senses sharpened, and my stomach did a somersault. I looked at one of my grenadiers, a private from Nicaragua named Roger Paguaga. His dark eyes looked like a pair of eight balls.

I swiveled in the direction of the cockpit and the door gunners as best I could, buried under people and equipment. I started yelling frantically at the guys closest to me to get the door gunner. My arm pumped repeatedly as I signaled what I wanted, my finger aimed at the shooter. My face must have been strained. I wanted to know how close I was to actual failure. The guy closest to the right-side door gunner tapped him and pointed at me. I mouthed at him, "What the fuck was that?"

He put both hands up to his mouth and called back to me over the roar of the engines, "Test fire . . . that was a test fire!"

I rolled my eyes. Then I checked to see if I'd pissed myself.

At over one hundred miles an hour we flew past craggy rocks and snow-filled canyons. As the pilots hugged the terrain, I pondered how much someone would pay to take this trip as a tourist. In places like this, places free of industrialization, the sky is such a deep blue that it almost blackens. At lower elevations I could see green trees. There were browns and whites and blues and blacks and greens. I got tapped on the shoulder. One of my soldiers held up five fingers and mouthed, "Five minutes!" I took a breath and then made the signal for those around me to lock and load. Then I pulled the charging handle back on my own M4 before allowing it to slam forward, chambering a round.

I stopped thinking about everything. There was nothing else in existence but the roar of the helicopter around me. Nikki no longer existed. My family no longer existed. I had no memories. I had no dreams, no plans for the future. It was all gone—as if the helicopter's vibrations had liquefied my soul, allowing it to evaporate in the rushing wind that brought combat closer with each passing second. My mind became a pure, blank slate, capable of only repeating a single mantra: *Go left, keep Taylor by your side, keep moving—no matter what. Go left, keep Taylor by your side, keep moving . . . .*

I felt the helicopter slowing, beginning its hover. It lurched and bucked before coming to rest on the side of a mountain. I still couldn't hear anything but the whine of the engines and the *whompwhomp* of the rotor blades. Then the tail gunner moved out of the way and I instinctively held my breath. The ramp began to lower, and light flooded the interior of the aircraft.

5

Shah-e-Kot Valley, Afghanistan

March 2002

I strained to see over the soldiers in front of me. They were struggling to shuffle off the bird as quickly as they could. I dragged my ruck across the floor of the aircraft in my right hand. In my left was my M4. I stepped off the ramp and started moving, completely disoriented.

Unexpectedly, all the air was sucked from my lungs. When we allowed for alpine elevations in the plan—about 9,500 feet—we tailored the helicopter load to the thin air and planned for freezing temperatures at the high altitude, but we hadn't planned for hauling such cumbersome gear on our backs. The first two steps off the bird were regular speed, the third was slower, and by the fourth step I was about to collapse. My head was spinning from trying to move too quickly with such a heavy pack. There wasn't enough oxygen in the air for me to do what I wanted to do. *Keep moving.* I couldn't get a satisfactory gulp of air. Suddenly my legs gave way and I dropped to a knee. *Keep moving.*

The first thought of which I became conscious was that I would live for at least a while longer. No one was shooting at me; nothing was exploding in my face. I looked around and saw that everyone else's movements had been grounded as well.

I scanned my surroundings on my knee, elbow resting on my ruck. We were in a bowl, surrounded by high ground on three sides. I then realized that other Rakkasans had us encircled— that they were our cover. Their uniforms were soiled and crinkled; their faces dirty and unshaven. They were part of the original group that been out there for seventy-two hours, but they looked as though they'd been out there a month. They were the most beautiful people I'd ever seen.

Still trying to catch my breath, I took my ruck and began to haul it across the open area. By the time I got to Captain K. I was trying not to hyperventilate. When I plopped down, I looked out at the opening of the bowl. I could see a valley, and mountains on the horizon. My watch said 5:35 p.m. I gazed up at the craggy ledges looming over me, and then to the cobalt blue sky above them. I paused, struck for a moment by the sheer rugged beauty of the place. Then I turned away. On the other side of the high ground, in the distance, I could hear sounds that seemed surreal. *Whoomp. Whoomp. Whoomp.* Bombs, detonating to the south, sounded like the footfalls of some mythic giant striding through the mountains. I could hear the faint crackle of gunfire. This was the real deal.

Captain K. was saying something. I wasn't listening. I was catching my breath and still marveling at the fact the LZ had been secure. I only turned to look at him when I heard my name. He wanted my platoon to lead the company south. I nodded and stood up.

We had no need to look at the grid coordinate for our destination. As long as we kept the thuds and pops to our front, and as long as they were getting louder, we would be headed in the right direction.

I told Sergeant David Reid to put Pascoe up front. Sergeant Joe Pascoe was the platoon "survivalist." A stocky ex-Marine, Pascoe was the guy who could make fire. He could capture, kill, and cook his own food and he could make his way through the woods effortlessly. Later, in Kandahar, he would design and build a trebuchet out of spare parts capable of launching six-packs of milk fifty yards. On the other hand, Pascoe could probably not help you match your drapes.

We had been in the bowl for ten minutes. The sky was still a deep blue, almost indigo, but the sun was starting to set and shadows were getting long. I looked up into the blue. Thousands of feet above me I saw the gray outline of an American B-52 headed south. Its four distinctive contrails stretched back as far as I could see. At that altitude, it was silent. I held my gaze on the plane as it traced a path toward the distant sounds of thunder. I had spent hours as a kid watching the B-52s based near my hometown in Louisiana. They had always been there in the sky for me, as a backdrop to my youth—at baseball games, down by the riverfront, stopped at a red light. You could rarely look to the sky in Shreveport and not see one. They were huge, powerful, and could carry nuclear weapons in their bomb bays. But they had always landed in a place I wasn't allowed to go. Perhaps that's why they hypnotized me.

In middle school, my classmates and I had watched them return from the first Gulf War. On that day, they had done a fly-by of Shreveport, flying low and slow over the city to the cheers of thousands. In a strange coincidence, I was now watching one of the same planes that I had seen as a kid. Only now it was on an actual attack run.

As I stared at it flying over the nearest ridge, I knew that it was seeing them, hearing their roar as an impressionable kid, that made me reply to the recruiter. Back then I hadn't really known the difference between the Army and the Air Force, but I knew I wanted to be a part of it. Now I could feel them leading me again, this time into a battle. Still spellbound by their power, I followed willingly.

As the plane flew out of sight, I dropped my gaze back to the jagged surroundings. Then I heard Captain K.: "Friedman, get us out of here."

Weighted down to a point that nearly buckled the knees, Sergeant Pascoe picked up his heading and we started south. We crested the bowl and began walking down a slight slope. As we walked down the hill, the sun dropped behind the high ground, leaving us in shadows.

We trudged on in the twilight, listening to the constant thud of impacting bombs. Not ten minutes later I saw all the right arms in front of me lift in the L-shaped signal for a halt.

"1-6, this is 1-2, over." It was Sergeant Reid. "You need to come up here and check this out."

I motioned to Taylor and we waddled to the front. Sergeant Pascoe stood facing south, overlooking a ravine two hundred feet across and probably fifty feet deep. Reid and Pascoe both looked at me. "Whaddya think, sir?" asked Sergeant Pascoe.

My response was the response of any true leader in time of trouble: "Ahhh, fuck."

"We could go through it, but I think we can skirt it to the left on that high ground," he said pointing. "It'd take longer, but I think it'd be easier on everybody than the going up and down would be."

I looked at Sergeant Reid. "What do you think?" I asked.

"I think Sergeant Pascoe's right, sir. I think it's a better idea to go around. I think that walking into that hole with all this weight would be a stupid idea."

"Okay," I said. "I think you're right. Keep moving around it. Let's go."

As I knew it would, the company net came to life. "Sir, they wanna know what the holdup is," Taylor informed me. I knew that was coming—it was what I'd wanted to avoid by making a quick decision.

"Tell 'em 'no holdup.' Tell 'em 'we're moving.' "

"Roger, sir."

Sergeant Pascoe led the company in a slow, winding curve toward the edge of the ravine. Within minutes Captain K., known simply as "Six" on the radio, was calling on the company net. He was in the middle of the company formation, probably a hundred yards back.

"1-6, this is Six, you're going the wrong way. Stop moving," came the Voice over the net.

"This is 1-6, roger, we're going around a large ravine. 1-2 and his team leader have a route picked out that we think'll be quicker than going down into the low ground, over," I explained.

"Roger, stop moving. Your platoon is going the wrong way, over."

"Roger, I know. We're moving around the ravine. Do you

want us go into it?" I asked.

"1-6, this Six, stop. You're going the wrong way. You're going east. We need to be headed south, over."

I looked from Taylor to Sergeant Reid to Sergeant Pascoe and back to Taylor. Holding the radio handset attached to Taylor's ruck, I looked at Sergeant Reid. "Is he serious? Really, is he even listening to me?"

"1-6, this is Six, has your platoon halted movement yet?" the Voice asked.

"Roger, we're stopped," I said.

"This is Six, roger, I want your platoon to hold its position while the formation passes on your right. 3rd Platoon will be taking the lead. I want your platoon to fall in behind 2nd Platoon in the rear. We're headed south from here."

In the remaining twilight I looked at Taylor, Reid, and Pascoe. They were shaking their heads with looks of exasperation that probably mirrored my own.

"This is 1-6, roger, I understand that we're to follow 2nd and 3rd Platoons into the ravine."

"This is Six, roger, your platoon was headed east."

Fifty feet deep. Steep. Rocky. Well over a hundred pounds on our backs. I might as well have been talking to my M4. I called Sergeant Collins on the ICOM and told him that we'd essentially been fired. All I heard on the other end was a, "Pfff." In my mind I could see his scrunching facial features, along with the shrug, and the headshake.

Stepping gingerly into the chasm I could feel loose gravel along with some larger, fist-sized rocks beneath my boots. It was a decline of about forty-five degrees, so at times I could balance myself by grabbing the ground above me. I had just stepped in, and I could already hear the muffled sounds of soldiers falling in front of me. I had almost reached the bottom when I heard someone go down above me. I turned around, straining to see through the green of the night vision monocle over my left eye. Several soldiers were trying to help another up.

I heard Sergeant Reid's voice over the ICOM. He said that one of his SAW gunners had gone down.

"Who is it?" I asked.

It was a specialist named Boudreau and now I was being told that he couldn't walk. *For the love of God, not now*, I thought.

"How bad is it," I asked.

Sergeant Reid came back, "I don't know yet. We're trying to get him up. He says he's twisted his knee and can't walk, over."

Then Sergeant Collins entered the conversation. "1-2, tell him to get the fuck up! There ain't no truck behind us to pick up the fallouts. And we can't carry his shit." He paused. "Over."

He was right. Unless there was bone sticking out of Boudreau's leg, Boudreau was going to have to march and keep up. In the infantry, "march or die" is a common expression. This is where it comes from.

While Boudreau pondered why he had ever joined the infantry in the first place, I called Captain K. on the company net and told him we were stopped in the back. The company first sergeant, who was now alongside Captain K. trying to navigate out of the gorge, came on the net. "Tell him nobody's going to pick his ass up! Tell him he *has* to march! He doesn't have a choice!" He said it in a low, tactical voice over the radio, but the exclamation points were understood.

It was completely dark when we crested the top of the gorge. We had lost nearly fifteen minutes with Boudreau, in what became a thirty-minute negotiation of the draw by the company. From there we found more level terrain, between the valley on our right and a massive ridge on our left.

The joy of being able to carry my overloaded ruck on easier terrain was soon overshadowed by the fact that it was getting more difficult by the minute. When carrying an excessive load on your back, the first body parts to go are your trapezius muscles. Most people assume just by virtue of the fact that you're walking, that the legs go first, but that's not true. The weight is literally hanging off your traps and they begin to burn. First you try to shift the shoulder straps of the ruck closer to your neck. This feels better for a minute or two, and then it begins to hurt worse. Then you try to spread the straps further out over your shoulders. This method of carrying forces you to stand up straight as opposed to walking hunched over. It lasts a little longer, but in the end, it too becomes painful. At that point, you begin to conjure up all the reasons why the company might need to stop—map check, recon ahead, whatever. Anything that would allow you to take off your ruck for a few seconds. You begin hoping for any reason, really. In the end, you just keep shifting your straps across your shoulder blades, from neck to shoulder. And you keep walking.

The weight and awkwardness nearly made me forget I was at over nine thousand feet and couldn't breathe normally. We marched for hours this way, listening to the rhythmic sound of falling bombs.

It wasn't like the walk past the Apaches earlier in the day, earlier in my life. My adrenaline valve was jammed in the open position, blessing me with a pleasant, low-level euphoria. I coupled that with extreme terror and uncertainty and called it even. I became eerily calm. On account of the odd combination of external stimuli, all the fear I felt earlier had mysteriously dissipated. I was no longer concerned with my apprehension and only mildly aware of the physical discomfort. Everything felt totally natural. Nothing seemed out of the ordinary. The booms, thuds, and crashes were getting closer with every step but it didn't seem to matter to me anymore. There was a strange sense of déjà vu—like I'd always been there.

Somehow I managed to stay focused on the guys in the platoon and how they were holding up, too. In fact, I can't recall a time when I felt *more* focused on the things going on around me. And yet, I still felt completely at ease—as if the years of Army training had worked. It was like being pulled in opposite directions by two very different drugs—one a stimulant, one a downer. My senses were being expanded beyond the normal human range.

If you're not careful under such exhausting physical stress, the emotions and chemicals drifting in and out of your brain can make a you numb; then the numbness becomes fatigue. In the infantry, we call it "droning." Droning is where you're technically still awake—you're walking and maybe you can answer questions to a degree—but in reality, you're brain has passed out. I can remember an all-night march during a training exercise—a "march to daylight" as we called it—where I started dreaming during the walk. I was sleeping, but my body was continuing on without me. It's a peculiar state in which to work, but once you've done it a few times it becomes less disconcerting. After a couple of years, your body adjusts, and it rarely, if ever, happens any more. It's usually younger, newer guys who drone.

This is what happened to Pfc. Peter O'Brien as we marched to the tune of two-thousand-pound bombs hitting mountains. O'Brien was from south Boston and had the Irish tattoos to match his name and the accent to match his hometown. He was twenty-two years old and married with two kids. O'Brien was also one of the few soldiers willing to speak up on behalf of all the lower enlisted guys. It seemed as though he could never be bothered with the whole "rank structure" thing, and he never allowed it to get in the way of telling those above him (from squad leader to company commander) when things were getting stupid. He was the platoon bellwether.

To that end, he had perfected the art of being a smartass complainer, but also of making his points convincing enough that he stayed out of trouble. Because his complaints were always valid, and because he always did a good job in handling his SAW, Sergeant Collins let it slide. And it wasn't that he was just a smartass; it was that he was so deadpan about it. Most of the time in Pakistan people couldn't tell if he was serious or not, me included. Like the time he held a PT formation for a squad of dead crickets.

We'd had a cricket infestation for a time in Jacobabad. One night, while walking the thin line between exhaustive boredom and actually losing it, O'Brien went about collecting a batch of the dead insects. By the time I was told about what was going on, Drill Sergeant O'Brien was well into his best *Full Metal Jacket* impression.

First I saw O'Brien's real squad standing in a semicircle. They looked like they didn't know whether to laugh or run for help. Then I saw what he was doing.

The dead crickets were arrayed in a crisp, disciplined formation on the floor. O'Brien, resting on one knee, hovered threateningly over them. With a blank expression on his face, he was yelling at them.

"What the fuck is wrong with you?" he bellowed at one lifeless insect. "Are you falling out of my formation!? Get the fuck back in my formation!"

Standing behind O'Brien, I looked up at his squad members. They looked back at me, still unsure as to whether or not this was funny. O'Brien continued ranting.

"Okay, that's it! You're all gonna pay now! The push-up position, ready, move!"

He started counting a cadence. "One, two, three . . . one, two, three . . . one, two, three! Hey, I said go all the way down, turd! Oh, you don't like push-ups? We'll do flutter-kicks! On your backs!"

I was going to stop him, but I just stood there, watching. At that point O'Brien took one finger and began flipping each dead cricket onto its back, one at a time. "The fluuuutter-kick! Ready, move! Keep kicking or you'll all pull twelve hours of guard duty tonight!"

That was enough. I tapped him on the shoulder and he stopped midsentence. "Hey," I said, looking down at him. "Come out here with me for a second."

"But sir, we're having a formation. They've been fucking up lately and now they're paying for it, sir. Can it wait?" His voice was completely earnest when he said this to me, his eyes pleading.

"Okay, I understand, but I want you to come talk to me out here."

I told him to get rid of the crickets and go to bed. I told him he might be disturbing to the newer guys. After a short but spirited resistance, he relented.

* * *

Time had ceased to exist in the traditional sense. There were hands on a clock. When they reached a certain point, we had to have a landing zone secured. The hands on my watch had made more than a few loops when Sergeant Dougherty called me on my ICOM. He informed me that O'Brien had gone down and that they were stopped, trying to get him up. I said okay and then told Sergeant Reid's squad to slow to a shuffle. Dougherty called back after about forty-five seconds and reported that O'Brien was up and moving.

Almost immediately after that he called me again. "Tell 'em to hold up. He's gone down again."

Out of curiosity, I decided to walk back and see what the problem was. By the time I got to O'Brien, he was on his feet and we had started advancing again. While Sergeant Dougherty led the rest of the squad, I figured I would trail O'Brien for a while to see what was up. I hadn't been following him for a minute when he took a sharp right turn and cut directly in front of me, nearly knocking me over. I grabbed him before he made it off the road.

"Hey man," I said, "where're you going?"

"I'm . . . I'm following the road," he slurred.

"No you're not. You just turned right and headed straight for the high ground," I said.

He came back: "I'm following the road."

He was done. His brain had paid the check, left a tip, and headed north. I had seen this before. It had happened to me at an army school. I kept losing my place in a march one night. Frantically, I had tried to find my squad. One of the other soldiers had put me back where I was supposed to be.

Immediately I noticed that the formation wasn't moving. After a few seconds I got lost again and set off to find my squad. This time the same soldier placed me back where I was supposed to be. Again, I noticed that the formation was stopped. It wasn't until the next day that I learned that the entire company had never moved in the time I kept "getting lost." I had only imagined that they'd moved on without me, and I'd been the only one walking around in a panic.

This is where O'Brien was. "Hey man," I said. "Look at me. Do you know where you are?" Dougherty suddenly appeared out of the green to examine his patient.

"I'm walkin'."

Dougherty put both hands on him, pointed him in the right direction, and said, "That way. Go that way."

O'Brien complied with the order. Sergeant Dougherty went back to guide the rest of the squad, but I remained with O'Brien. Five minutes later he went down again. His legs had just given out. He lay there in a heap of arms and legs and equipment. He wasn't moving. I couldn't tell, but he looked to be unconscious. I looked in the direction of the nearest soldier. In a tactical, whisper voice, I yelled, "Hey, I need some help getting him up!" No response. The soldier kept walking. I looked at the next soldier and said the same thing. Again, no response. He too walked right past me. Then I realized what was going on. The idea of having to stop your momentum, bend down, and lift up something heavy was just too much. The thought was heartbreaking. The guys that walked past me knew that if I didn't use their names, they could feign ignorance of the situation. The next person I saw was Sergeant Divona, my forward observer.

"Sergeant Divona, stop. I need some help pickin' this guy up."

"I . . ." he said. "I . . ." And then he gave in. He knew he was caught.

The next soldier in line was a grenadier in O'Brien's squad. I called out his name. Nothing. He kept walking. "Hey, goddammit, c'mere! We need some help!" I whisper-yelled. That time the grenadier responded.

Fatigue was setting in. We had been walking for hours. Guys were hauling their rucks with sheer will power alone. My neck was killing me. My NODs and Kevlar helmet were weighing my head down and I couldn't stretch it. If I tried to crane my head back, my helmet hit my ruck and the back plate in my vest. And now the cold was beginning to exact a toll. I could feel my hands going numb. I was only wearing a thin set of cotton gloves, and now I was having trouble moving my fingers. I could see my breath through the night vision. Fortunately, my torso was kept warm by my body armor. It was a strange sensation, in that while my exposed fingers slowly froze, I could feel sweat running down my chest beneath my plates.

To make matters worse, the smooth ground disappeared and we started up an incline. I had been walking for a few minutes, one foot, then the next foot, when I felt a crunch underneath my boot. It wasn't an "oh shit I broke something" crunch. It was another kind of crunch that I recognized—only it took a second for it to register. I looked down and focused my NODs on the ground.

The snow line.

For a brief moment I had a flash of sanity and thought to myself, *What the fuck is a Nintendo-playing suburban kid doing in the*

Hindu Kush at nine thousand feet, marching in the snow toward the sound of guns? I seemed to have forgotten that once in my life I had pined jealously for this opportunity.

Plodding up the slope, I looked back. The moon had risen, giving us very good visibility. Behind me I viewed the latter half of my platoon, stretched out over a hundred yards. The formation had begun to curve around to the right, so I could look over my shoulder and easily see the trailing soldiers. I couldn't make out facial features, but I could identify each soldier's silhouette simply by his height, weight, or gait. I could make out Sergeant Bryce Beville's second gun team. Pfc. Terrence Kamauf was the most recognizable, carrying the M240 machine gun. It was slung over his shoulders and it hung horizontally at his waist. Kamauf was the tallest guy in the platoon and, carrying the longest weapon, he looked like a moving plus sign. Walking beside him was Private Kyle Johnson, the smallest soldier in the platoon. Johnson's ruck weighed more than he did. Kamauf's ammunition bearer, Pfc. John Smerbeck, rounded out the team and walked beside the other two stoically.

Looking forward again, I watched Taylor pacing beside me in silence. All I could hear was labored breathing. Suddenly I heard what had become the unmistakable sound of someone falling. I looked over my shoulder in time to see Johnson flailing on the ground. I saw that two mortar rounds had fallen out of his ruck and were now rolling down the hillside. The eighteen-inch cardboard casings in which the mortars were packed rolled without hesitation to the bottom of the hill. They bounced over loose rocks and snow before disappearing into the darkness. It was as if they had waited patiently for this moment, and were now making their escape from the interminable march.

My first thought upon losing the rounds was horror. A second later, it turned to, "Ahhh, fuck it." All anyone could muster was a wistful glance into the darkness of the low ground.

Gasping, I continued walking up the craggy, snow-covered slope. I was thinking about how fortunate I had been to have not yet fallen, when my foot, weighted down and fatigued, failed to clear a rock jutting up from the ground. I pitched forward, the weight of my equipment forcing me face first into the snow. My M4 was flung from my hands, landing several feet away from me. As I fell forward, my rucksack hit my helmet, knocking it off my head. As my face met the snow, my ruck came to rest on the back of my head and shoulder blades—all one hundred and some-odd pounds of it. In that precarious position, I couldn't move. My arms were pinned and I couldn't even push myself up. I managed a muffled, "Help, I can't move." The two guys nearest me lifted the ruck from off my head, and I crawled to all fours.

After walking for nearly eleven straight hours, we crested a rise in the frozen earth and found ourselves on a field of battle. We were exhausted, filthy, and out of breath. War had come barging into our houses on September the 11. And now, in the early hours of a March morning in 2002, for us at least, it had come full circle.

Before us stood the twelve-thousand-foot peak, Takhur Gar. Now known as Objective Ginger, it had become the site of the fiercest fighting of the battle. It was no longer on TV or in a scale model. It was real. I simply had two initial thoughts on seeing this mountain that was less than a thousand yards away from where I stood. My first thought was: *That's a big fucking mountain.* My second was: *It's on fire.* There were trees with branches burning all along the north face of Takhur Gar. I'm not sure if Captain K. consciously decided to stop, was ordered to stop, or just did it instinctively, but we did. I took a knee with Taylor at my side. Just then a bomb hit the side of the mountain, lighting up the entire sky.

I had never before seen anything like that. I had never witnessed a shot fired in anger, much less, a bomb fall on people. When the bomb hit, the sound was deafening. It made the air vibrate. For the split second in which the mountainside was alight from the explosion, I could see trees swaying from the shockwave. I could see embers blowing off branches and into the snow. Kneeling, I watched as two more bombs struck the mountain in quick succession, causing the same set of effects. It was then that I noticed Sergeant Collins had moved forward from the back of the column. He was kneeling next to me. When he saw me looking at him through my night vision, he pointed to the mountain. Then he whispered, measuring out each word carefully, "A man's got to know his limitations." I assumed he was talking about the terrorists. With each impact I ducked my head reflexively.

After a minute or two of watching this lightshow, Taylor handed me the radio. Captain K. was calling me to the front of the formation.

This was our destination. He told me that my platoon was to form the southernmost sector of our perimeter and that I was also responsible for setting up and securing the LZ for the incoming Chinook. At the time we had an hour remaining.

In order to set in the company, Captain K. wanted to conduct a reconnaissance of the area ahead. He picked me to go with him since it was going to be my area. A minute later we set out.

During the march, high ground to our right had prevented us from seeing the Shah-e-Kot Valley. It was on the other side of this high ground from which we had heard the sound of constant thunder as bombs devastated the valley and the villages of Serkhankel, Marzak, and Babulkul within. Captain K. and I walked briskly up a rise, and up ahead I could see an area where it appeared the high ground was tapering off. When we reached the break, I got my first look at the valley I'd come so far to see.

What I saw was fire and brimstone. It was Dante's *Inferno*. Less than eight hundred yards away from me, bombs were raining down on the valley. The sky was falling on those who had brought war to America. Entire payloads of gravity bombs fell and exploded in fantastic bursts of orange, yellow, and white. Two-thousand-pound satellite-guided bombs struck, reverberating throughout the valley. Cluster bombs fell, detonating on contact like a hundred hand grenades. Shrapnel was swirling like confetti. The air became metal. For a moment, Captain K. and I just stood there, taking it all in. On the edge of the abyss, we gazed down into a churning sea of fire. The attack was strangely hypnotic; the fury and intensity—overwhelming.

It was a vulgar display of power. It was unrestrained collective rage. But if anyone, anywhere had ever deserved such punishment, then this was the time, this was the place.

Whether the number of al Qaeda terrorists in the valley was large or small, I would never know. But I do know that the ones caught in the crossfire picked up the tab for the ones who weren't there. Whether or not they had been involved in the planning for 9/11, whether or not they thought it had been a good idea, they paid. That night, thousands of pounds worth of iron fragmentation and concussion rendered them square with the house.

It was payback. And I was okay with that.

For some reason I seem to remember turning and running even before I saw the brilliant flash. Either way, before the sound and shockwave reached us, we had turned and were running back in the direction of the company. Neither of us had said anything. Our movements were reflexive. The sound was earsplitting and, like in nightmares, I felt I couldn't move rapidly enough. As we ran with bursting lungs, I heard within feet of me, the sound, *ffffth*—as searing hot metal sliced into the earth.

This was the edge of the kill zone.

We finished marking the LZ with only minutes to spare. When it was done, Sergeant Collins sat next to me and, shivering together, we watched the deconstruction of Takhur Gar continue. I could no longer see directly into the valley, but I could still see the flashes of light and hear the thunderous booms from within. The planes above pummeled the mountain and valley without respite. Sitting there wide-eyed, I didn't see how anyone on the receiving end of the onslaught could survive.

Slowly starting to freeze, I sat back and watched the show. I thought of the movie *The Big Lebowski*. In it, John Goodman's character, Walter Sobchak, is smashing his nemesis' Corvette with a crowbar.

I hear him yelling at the top of his lungs, "Do you see what happens, Larry? Do you see what happens when you fuck a stranger in the ass?"

He brings the crowbar down over his head and onto the windshield of the pristine car, crushing it. "This is what happens, Larry!" He strikes the hood of the car. "This is what happens when you fuck a stranger in the ass!*" He swings the crowbar squarely into the driver's-side door.*

Yes, Walter, this is what happens. This is what happens. I listened in the cold night air, as bombs, a few football fields away, continually found their marks.

Minutes later I heard the faint thumping of rotors echoing through the mountains. Shortly thereafter, the Chinook landed on our LZ. I sat motionless, with my back to my ruck, watching through my NODs as grainy green figures exited the back of the bird. With the night vision, I could see the two infrared targeting lasers used by the door gunners, as they anxiously scanned the surrounding terrain. The bird remained there, rotors spinning, for less than three minutes, while the last of 3rd Platoon's troops shuffled off the ramp. Once the last man cleared it, the Chinook's rotor blades deepened in tone. At that point, wind, dust, and pebbles were scattered through the air in a blast of wind as the bird rose into the night sky. Seconds later everything was quiet. Even the bombing had stopped.

We still had a little less than an hour before daylight. Curled up and trying to retain warmth in any way possible, I began to doze. For the second night in a row, I lay on the ground with my teeth chattering. I wasn't aware of the existence of any plan past sunrise. All I knew was that I would live for another night, and at dawn, in some form or fashion, we would take the fight to the enemy.

Part II

KNOWLEDGE

"That's the attractive thing about war," said Rosewater. "Absolutely everybody gets a little something."

—Kurt Vonnegut, *Slaughterhouse-Five*

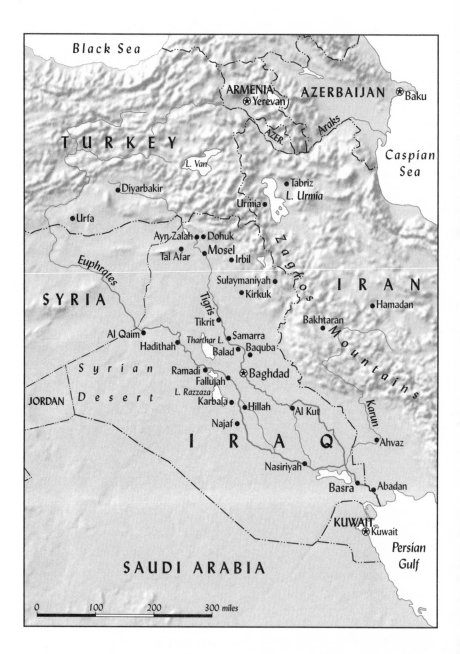

6

The Desert

March 2003

I awoke with a start in Kuwait, covered in sweat. I had been napping in the front seat of my humvee. I decided to step out onto the desert floor and stretch my legs. The constriction of my chemical protective suit was bothersome, but I was being forced to wear it anyway. At the time apparently, someone thought Iraq had chemical weapons.

I leaned over the hood of the truck, resting my elbows on it. I scanned the area briefly before settling my gaze on the western horizon. The road stretching out before me was black-top. It disappeared in the distance some miles before it reached the horizon. I'd never before stood on land so flat. Besides the thin strip of black there were only two other colors in the land-scape to my front. One was the haze color of an empty sky that was neither blue nor gray. The other was the light beige, almost off-white, color of the endless desert. The two colors met at the horizon, nearly blending. To look in that direction was to squint.

To my back was a silent armada of vehicles. Some were gun trucks and some were command trucks. Some were troop transports and others were refuelers. In all, they represented the 3rd Brigade Combat Team of the 101st Airborne Division—the Rakkasans.

Before us, at the still unseen point where the sky met the land, was the Iraqi frontier. Behind us was Afghanistan and everything else.

Having decided to take a walk, I ended up sitting with Lieutenant Colonel Ahuja in a humvee, where we discussed the merits of invading versus not invading—and what we thought we could expect. Ahuja was a former Rakkasan on the division staff, still several months away from taking command of his first battalion in the 101st. In our conversation, the roles were oddly reversed—the soon-to-be battalion commander (who wasn't all that far from retirement) was asking the young lieutenant what combat had been like in Afghanistan. Despite that, I sensed that he recognized what lay ahead; he knew what was just over the horizon. Unlike those who'd sent us there in the first place, Ahuja had spent his entire adult life preparing for this moment. He looked me straight in the eye while we sat there, and said something to me with the expression of a guy who thought, *You may think I'm crazy for saying this, but I know what I'm talking about.*

"You know, Lieutenant Friedman, everybody keeps talking about how all the Iraqis are gonna surrender, and how this is just gonna be a walk in the park. But I'm not so sure. People don't like being invaded. They don't like being bombed, and they don't like tanks in their streets—even if they do live under a dictator. That's just reality. I think there's always gonna be that guy who's out to fight for his country no matter what. He doesn't care about the politics. He just knows that we're invading *his* country. And he knows he's gonna to do everything in his power to stop us."

I thought about it and just said, "Sir, I hope you're wrong."

We had moved out from Camp New Jersey the day before. It had been a day of missile exchanges and confused radio reports, but we hadn't really played any significant part at all. I had had projectiles launched at me and then, after nightfall, I had listened to the buzz of Tomahawk cruise missiles flying directly over my head on their way across the border. For all its buildup, "shock and awe" to me had been a surprisingly soft mechanical buzz a hundred feet over my head.

Around three o'clock that afternoon Colonel Ahuja and I went to recon the border with Iraq. We were supposed to find the general who was coordinating the division's passage through the breach lane.

For some reason I had pictured explosions as being part of breaching the heavily guarded border between the two countries. Perhaps some running and screaming Iraqi border guards. But when we arrived at the border, the scene was calm and businesslike. There were U.S. Army humvees parked up against a twelve-foot-high dirt berm. There were also several SUVs belonging to the Kuwaiti border patrol. On the other side, I was told, was a unit of combat engineers. They were carefully deconstructing the dirt berms and wire obstacles that marked the entrance into Iraq. There was no hint of resistance.

My vision of tanks crashing through heavily fortified watchtowers was quickly replaced with the reality of an orderly preparation for the smooth transit of thousands of soldiers from the 3rd Infantry Division and the 101st Airborne Division into enemy territory. Everything was so *nonchalant.*

When we returned to the brigade assembly area, I spent the rest of the afternoon taking pictures with friends and dozing. I would normally have spent the time going over the battle plan with my NCOs, but in this case no plan had yet filtered down to our level.

The mission was simply to drive to a point on the map and once there, to wait for instructions. The point on the map was twenty miles southwest of Najaf, some 240 miles into Iraq. It was called FARP Shell—and it was simply a plot of desert destined to be used as a forward area refueling and rearming point for the division's Apache helicopters. The name Shell came from the gas station, the FARP being our improvised desert equivalent. The two other FARPs being established in southern Iraq were FARP Conoco and FARP Exxon. Read into that what you want.

I had been given a stack of maps and a sheet with typed grid coordinates that were supposed to keep us on track as we drove. I knew nothing about the cities and areas through which we would pass, and I knew nothing about possible enemy contact along the route. The whole thing had an air of, "Fuck it. Drive toward Najaf and see if anybody tries to stop you."

When we crossed the border into Iraq that night there was no fanfare. There were no hurrahs or clapping or fireworks. It wasn't even combat as I'd remembered it. It was just driving.

At night. In Iraq.

If anything, it had the feel of a ride at an amusement park—either a roller coaster or a haunted house. That feeling of right after you're strapped in and you start moving—the feeling of "Oh well . . . guess there's no going back now." There was that and there was also the slight nagging feeling that I didn't know where in the hell I was going.

I stayed up all night with a little green flashlight, poring over all the maps and charts as we drove.

After daybreak I could see that we were in Bedouin territory. Every few miles we would pass an encampment of their patchwork tents. For the first time in weeks there was vegetation. In this area the desert was dotted with fixed tumbleweed-looking bushes. It wasn't real vegetation, it wasn't even green for that matter, but it was plant life nonetheless. I was beginning to forget what any landscape other than desert looked like—it had been weeks since I'd seen anything other than flatness and sand.

That night we stopped the convoy outside of Busayyah. We had been driving for nearly twenty-four straight hours and hadn't slept. No one seemed to know the protocol for resting a convoy during an invasion, so we simply pulled off to the side of the road, made a guard roster, and then went to sleep. I stayed in my truck and just leaned over. Sergeant Croom dismounted his truck, pulled out his sleeping bag, and went to bed on the shoulder of the road.

We spent two days making our way through the blank desert, stopping only once to rest. As a foreign desert caravan, we cautiously passed through the periphery of towns, wary of the inhabitants who stood by the roadside and stared. We sifted through false reports of enemy contact ahead and had a confrontation over the right of way during a traffic jam with 3rd Infantry Division tanks. As with all major military maneuvers since the beginning of time, this one too was defined by dust and confusion.

When we arrived at FARP Shell after the second day, darkness had fallen. The only light visible to the naked eye was starlight. I stepped out onto the desert floor and looked into the sky. As if on cue, rockets began lighting up the distant night sky. Being so far away, they seemed to ascend slowly in a silent, upward arc, blooming and spreading in a single group—each yellow pinpoint climbing, flickering, and then disappearing. They were flying in the direction of Najaf.

I became strangely at peace with the situation. I was neither happy nor sad, neither confident nor frightened. There just didn't seem to *be* anything else. This was all there was, this was all I was: a single entity standing in the desert, surrounded by chaos that I could not touch and that could not touch me. It was Anaconda all over again: I was numb. I had no past and no future. I was in my element.

The fear and the adrenaline—they both come together on a battlefield when the rounds aren't landing too close yet. Surrounded on all sides by death and destruction, you are still whole. You are the opposite of dead. You feel the blood coursing through your veins, nourishing this aliveness. You sense death very near, you see it twinkling in the sky. You are as close to it as you can ever come without losing your mind—and yet you know it cannot touch you. You feel death's proximity and it makes you alive. You feel what it is to exist. It becomes something just as tangible as pain or orgasm.

I watched the glimmering lights trace across the sky for a while. *(Bodies are being torn apart. Families are being ruined.)* In the distance I could hear an occasional rumble; I could feel intermittent vibrations. There was *(flesh, bone, pooling blood, screaming)* nothing else.

And I felt nothing.

I awoke the next morning and found myself surrounded by the same vast emptiness that had followed us from Kuwait. Nothing had changed except the weather. Whereas I could usually see the sun creeping over the horizon, now the sky was a hazy gray. When I stepped out of my truck, the first thing I noticed was a stiff west wind.

A few minutes later, Sergeant Croom walked over to my truck. We were talking while at the same time offhandedly watching two of the guys dig our restroom some distance away from the humvees. The wind was beginning to whip around.

With no warning, a thunderous boom tore through the morning haze. I looked at Sergeant Croom with raised eyebrows and said, "Either that was big or that was close."

We stood there without moving for another few seconds, waiting for other impacts. Nothing happened. I was beginning to think that I would just ignore it, as it seemed to be gunfire that didn't concern me.

But that's when the Voice on the radio alerted us of an enemy mortar strike. I was told to gear up for a counterattack. While Croom hurried back to his truck, I wondered how anyone could have found us so far out in the middle of nowhere. Beyond that, I tried to figure out how they could have maneuvered so close to us in the open desert and gotten off a mortar round. As I threw on my vest and put on my helmet, I couldn't figure out why somebody would shoot just one mortar at us, and not start dropping round after round on us. Vaguely, I thought maybe their tube had broken.

Sergeant Croom came back in full gear. While we waited for somebody to tell us what to do, we started digging—just in case we needed the cover.

"At least the al Qaeda guys in Afghanistan knew how to use mortars," I told him. They really fucked up Charlie Company pretty bad. Nobody hurt, but still—I mean a lot of those guys are still jumpy around loud noises." I paused to scoop a shovelfull out of the hard earth. Then I continued. "And the thing about mortars is that you can't hear 'em coming like you can artillery shells or bombs."

"Aw, that's bullshit," Croom declared. "I've been on a training range and heard 'em fall near me. Who told you that shit?"

"Go ask anybody in Charlie," I said, "or shit, just ask Krueger. He was in Anaconda too. I'm just tellin' you," I said as I scooped, "that those guys said they couldn't hear any of 'em falling. And by the way, those were 82s those shitbirds were dropping."

He looked at me with a skeptic's raised eyebrow.

A short time later I received our mission over the radio. Our mission, the Voice explained, was to stand down. The distant boom had not been an enemy mortar. It had been an American F-16. Through the crackling radio traffic, I heard the Voice say, " . . . just fired a missile at our Patriot battery and took out a radar site."

I stuck my head out of the truck, looking for Sergeant Croom. "Hey, c'mere. You gotta hear this shit! An F-16 just took out one of the fuckin' Patriots!"

He said, "No shit? Anybody hurt?"

I hadn't thought that far ahead yet. "Uhh, I don't know. They didn't say anything about that."

But I was already losing focus on the current situation, now that the enemy threat was gone. My mind was beginning to drift back to another time and place. All the talk of falling mortars, and now, F-16s firing on friendly troops, was bringing back a flood of memories—memories of our first morning in Operation Anaconda.

An eerie quiet has descended upon the Shah-e-Kot Valley and its surrounding peaks. As the sky turns from black to purple to blue, I sit, unmoved, against my ruck. I am a small, living, breathing dot on a smoking expanse of desolation. The stillness is palpable. All I can hear are my own teeth chattering in the cold air. With the light comes sobriety, and Life itself seems a bit self-conscious about its behavior during the night. Eventually I will learn that the silence and calm following butchery is directly proportional to the amount of bloodletting that occurs.

I am groggy. I think that I must have dozed for nearly an hour because the night's events are already beginning to seem like a dream. I hear movement around me as guys who aren't pulling security start to wake from their short naps. As the sky begins to lighten, my heart sinks as I realize mountains buttress us to the east—mountains that will block our only source of heat for hours.

Sergeant Collins is next to me. We make some small talk as I scan our surroundings for the first time in the early morning light. Being in the low ground, I can't see much. The platoon is facing southwest, stretched in a defensive line spanning a hundred yards. They are on the reverse slope of a rise in the earth. I look for Charlie Company, but can't see them anywhere. In the night it had come across the net that they had been engaged in a firefight the day prior and are now somewhere on the high ground to our east.

I can see several guys changing their socks, while others brush off their weapons. Objective Ginger looms above them to the south. I have removed my set of equipment and it lies on the ground next to me. Sergeant Collins has taken off his helmet despite the cold. Having worn mine for over twelve straight hours, I decide to do the same, setting it gently on the ground by my ruck. My weapon lies in my lap. I can hear other quiet voices speak to each other in the growing light.

An inbound bullet is always felt before it is heard.

I twitch involuntarily as the first round streaks through the air above me, cutting a path through the thin mountain air. Breaking the silence, the crack is loud and nearly instantaneous. Later I find that this sensation is caused by the tiny sonic boomlet that accompanies whizzing bullets. I have never before been on the receiving end of any projectile other than baseballs or paintballs. At worst, those leave bruises, not holes. This is serious. This is a new thing for me.

I am awake.

I'm on a stage. The spotlight has just found me. Blinded, I try to cover my eyes. I look into the crowd. They are waiting. I am unprepared.

My brain clicks back on. I yell the obvious. "Sniiiiiiiper!" The call is echoed throughout the platoon. I hit the ground. On the way down, I snag my helmet. As I lie on my stomach shivering, I put it on and try to snap on the chinstrap with my nearly numb fingers. I can feel rocks digging into the palms of my hands as well as my knees. I try to flatten myself as much as possible. As a kid, I'd seen surprised squirrels do something similar to this in my neighborhood. Now I am doing my best imitation. It seems like the thing to do.

Complete thoughts slowly begin forming. That round came from behind us. What the fuck? Everyone else realizes the same thing and they are instinctively repositioning themselves to face the northwest.

Silence.

Then: "Who sees him?" I yell it. Another voice asks if anyone has been hit. Suddenly there is a jumble of "Who sees . . . I don't . . . anything . . . do you . . . what?" Words and sentences become tangled. As the squad leaders desperately try to glean from their men if anyone has seen anything, I look for Taylor. He has the radio.

I see him twenty feet away, but he may as well be on the moon. Sergeant Divona is with him. I start to crawl toward them, but I only get a few feet before I realize I don't have my load-bearing vest with my extra ammo magazines. I move quickly in reverse and grab it. I drag it behind me, knowing full well that sitting up on a knee to don it can mean a bullet in the head.

As I crawl, I become aware that my teeth are chattering—literally knocking together—in my head. I notice that I am still freezing. For some odd reason, I feel cheated. I had hoped that if I had to fight, I'd least have enough adrenaline pumping through me to ward off the cold. I feel that this isn't fair. It never happens like this on TV. On TV no one ever has to fight with teeth clanging and hands so cold they can barely operate the trigger on a gun. I had hoped a shootout would at least warm me up.

I am almost there when the second round pierces the air. I dig my face into the ground. Then I look up. I glance behind me, at most of the platoon. *"Did anybody see an impact?"* I shout. *Suddenly Rito Diaz, one of Sergeant Beville's machine gunners, calls out: "I just saw it hit behind me!"*

Sergeant Collins is scrambling on all fours toward Taylor and me. He looks at Diaz and asks, "Are you sure?"

"I . . . I think so, Sergeant," Diaz responds.

Fuck. Finally, I make it to Taylor and Sergeant Divona. All right. Think, think, think, goddammit. Okay. "Taylor, call it in to the CP. Tell 'em we're gonna engage the sniper. Sergeant Divona . . ." I stop, wheels turning furiously in my head. I look at him. "Hold up." I want to get a better look before I make another move. CRACK!!! Another round passes directly over my head. As with the others, I can feel it.

The call goes out from the platoon, "Is anybody hit?!" Nothing. No one has been hit. I am beginning to think that this is the world's worst sniper. Three shots have been fired at a stationary platoon with no hits. My next thought is a bit more cynical. If we've been so lucky on the first three, then it is only a matter of seconds before our luck will run out. Then someone calls out, "Can we shoot?!" This strikes me as an utterly stupid question. I yell as loud as I can, "Yes, goddammit! Light the motherfucker up!" Collins screams something similar at the same time.

He is next to me. "Come on, let's flank around to the left. Let's get up the hill and waste this motherfucker!" he urges me. It is the moment for which Collins has been waiting his entire life. He is actually going to get to close with and destroy an enemy. In his mind, I think, he has already charged up the hill, pulled out his bayonet, jammed it between the sniper's ribs, and watched his lifeblood run out.

"Hold . . . Hold up, man!" I say, worriedly. He has a look in his eyes that says if I hesitate, he will take the platoon and go on without

me. He is serious. At once I am concerned that the age-old power struggle between platoon leaders and platoon sergeants is about to reach a breaking point. In the six months we've known each other, we've never had a conflict over what is best for the platoon. It looks like that is about to change now. "NoNoNo! Wait," I plead. I am thinking again. I want to prop myself up on all fours to get a clearer look up the hill. For a second I think about the sense in that.

I do it anyway. I have to do something. I can't see anything. As I lower myself back into the prone position, I suddenly feel that aliveness—that by propping myself up to see, I've somehow cheated death by surviving. I can hear Sergeant Collins, "Sir, let's go!"

A fourth round cuts through the cold morning air, the loud crack echoing around in my brain. We try to get as close to the ground as we can. "I see him, I see him!" It is Pfc. Smerbeck. The next sound I hear is his M4. Smerbeck doesn't hesitate for a second in returning fire. "He just dropped out of sight!" Smerbeck calls out. The machine gunner next to him, Kamauf, turns to Sergeant Beville and asks, "Can I shoot?" Kamauf wants to unleash his heavy machine gun. No answer from Sergeant Beville. He is at a terrible vantage point and can't see anything. Then Beville, deliberately disregarding the danger, cracks a joke about Smerbeck screwing up the round count. After he says it, he looks at me, wide-eyed and grinning. Somebody asks Smerbeck if he's hit him, and Smerbeck answers in the negative, saying he doesn't think so.

I look at Sergeant Collins. "Wait. Let's prep it first." I shift my hips and turn to Sergeant Divona, my forward observer. "Hey man, call it in and have 'em drop some mortar rounds on the sniper." I realize we're way too close for mortars, but I don't care. I don't know if I have the stomach for an uphill assault. I pause for a second, waiting for Divona's retort. For the first time in four months, however, Sergeant Divona doesn't complain about the mission. He doesn't question it and he doesn't give me the usual look like I've just killed his dog. Relieved by his reaction, I watch as he goes to work on his radio. He is now calling in a strike with literally no margin for error.

It has been about a minute since Smerbeck returned fire and the sniper's rifle has fallen silent. This is good at least. Divona finishes with the radio call. For a few more moments we wait. It grows quiet again. I'm not breathing. Suddenly Taylor's radio comes to life. "Sir, it's for you. It's First Sergeant."

I take the handset from him and put it to my ear. First Sergeant wants to know the direction of the sniper and his distance from us. Have I not called that in to the CP already? Wasn't that the first thing I did? It is the first thing I should have done, anyway. I must have forgotten. "Roger," I answer, "it's a hundred meters at, uhh, fifty-five degrees, over." He repeats it back to me in confirmation and then there is silence.

I look at Divona, concerned. I ask him what the holdup is. He just frowns and shrugs. I glance back at the platoon. Everyone is still down, but their eyes are still trained intently on the sniper's position. No one speaks as we wait for the mortars to fall.

The radio crackles again. Taylor answers it and I see his eyes widen. I can't make out much, but I distinctly hear, "Cease fire! Cease fire!" come across. Taylor drops the handset to his side. "Sir," he says, "they're telling us to stop shooting immediately."

Perplexed, I ask him why. This makes no sense at all.

"Sir, they said it's a friendly grid. They said we just called in a mortar strike on our own scouts."

I am stunned momentarily. How can the scouts be that close to the sniper? That can't be. Wait a second. . . . A new thought begins to mate-

rialize in my rattled brain. "No. No," I shake my head. "Those rounds were close. . . . Diaz saw one impact behind him," I stammer. Jaw-dropping surprise does not begin to describe what I am feeling. If it's true . . . Words like "friendly fire" and "fratricide" begin to dance behind my eyes.

"No sir," Taylor says. "Battalion says that scout snipers are behind us and that they were engaging targets in the valley and they just reported being fired at."

I have now fumbled my platoon through our first combat action. I have ordered my soldiers to fire on their own scouts and asked my forward observer to drop mortars on these same soldiers. This is not my fault, but I can see that this type of work is not as easy as it looks on TV.

The F-16 missile that struck the Patriot battery at FARP Shell was a high-speed anti-radiation missile. The plane had been on its way to Baghdad when the Patriot site locked onto the jet, causing the pilot to fire on the battery. With the whipping wind and dust now obscuring visibility, he probably never saw the target at which he was firing.

After the mistaken attack, the strong winds started becoming more troublesome by the minute. By midafternoon we were in a full-blown dust storm. Visibility was rapidly dropping, and our latrine that consisted of four walls made of ponchos strung up to shovels was slowly being blown apart.

The whole platoon was buttoned up inside of the trucks. The humvees didn't really keep the dust out, but they did prevent you from being slapped in the face by little rocks zipping through the air. Listening to the chatter on the Division net, I started thinking of the rifle companies sitting in holes in the ground, out in the open desert. However miserable my platoon was, Collins and his guys were considerably worse off. It was then that the weather changed drastically.

The sky, the air, and the land all at once became orange. Within seconds it changed again, this time to a deep ruby red. Suddenly we were on an alien planet. Sand began buffeting the windows of the truck. I looked at my driver and asked, "*What the fuck is this?*" Then, without warning, we were swallowed completely by a wall of darkness.

It was a devouring blackness. I could feel a low vibration in everything around me. Day became night and I could no longer see my own hand in front of my face. I was only conscious of two senses—those of taste and touch. I could taste the sand, feel it in my mouth, between my teeth, in my throat. We were being buried alive.

Then it started to rain. But not real rain. Spheres of mud began falling from the still darkened sky, landing with thumps on the hood and windshield of my truck. They fell irregularly, as if the sky wanted to rain, but couldn't muster the strength to do so. The sand had consumed even the rain. At this moment, on a field of battle consisting of hundreds of square miles, armies, steeled for battle, ground to a halt.

It was as if the land knew what was happening. It knew our intentions, and it knew that this war, as with all wars, would end badly. It was as if the sky had opened, pouring sand into the gears of the war machines on both sides. It was the land's final, desperate attempt to stop the war from tak-

ing place. And if it couldn't, it would at least serve as a warning. A warning that darkness was coming—for Americans and
Iraqis alike.

From left to right: Sgt. 1st Class Jim Collins, 1st Lt. Sam Edwards, and me in Jacobabad, Pakistan.

Months of waiting around in Pakistan for a mission, coupled with long hours on radio watch, eventually took its toll on Specialist Taylor.

Taking up positions on the east side of the Shah-e-Kot Valley shortly after sunrise on our first day in Operation Anaconda. The cloud on the left is a bomb exploding half a mile away.

Takhur Gar—also known as Objective Ginger during Operation Anaconda—loomed over us. During our time in the Valley, al Qaeda fighters remained dug in on the mountain.

Two soldiers from my platoon stay low as the bombs fall on the Shah-e-Kot Valley. An al Qaeda truck—caught in the previous day's fighting—lies burned out in the low ground.

Shortly before our extraction from the Shah-e-Kot Valley. Clockwise from left to right: Spc. Jose Limon, Sgt. Joseph Pascoe, Spc. Michael "Doc" Rojas, Sgt. Josh Nantz, me, Staff Sgt. David Reid, Spc. Jason Boudreau, and Pfc. Kyle Walter.

Flying into the Zhawar Kili area near the Afghan/Pakistan border. Two weeks after Operation Anaconda we went there to clear a cave complex. *Photo courtesy T. Kamauf*

Always the social one, Specialist Kamauf practiced unit-level diplomacy with a serious-looking Afghan fighter who wore a borrowed American helmet for the photo. *Photo courtesy T. Kamauf*

At Zhawar Kili, we had the privilege of working closely with Afghan anti-Taliban fighters. I am standing at the top left, while Sgt. Joe Pascoe is squatting in the middle.

A ruined, thousand year-old caravanserai lies in the open desert some 30 miles southwest of Najaf, on the old road between Baghdad and Mecca. We found it while operating a defensive screen on the southern edge of FARP Shell.

From left, Phil Dickinson and me. Sheltering a "caravan" for the first time in hundreds of years, the Delta Company command post and radio antenna can be seen outside of what remained of the northern wall of the caravanserai (roadside inn).

Three Chinooks flying low over the desert, twelve miles southwest of Baghdad. We staged there for half a day before moving on the city.

Sitting on the south bank of the Tigris in Baghdad's Daura neighborhood, this crumbling Baath Party mansion sustained two bomb strikes in the early stages of the invasion. By the time we entered it, nothing was left inside but rubble and debris. Everything else had been looted.

After clearing the Daura oil refinery, Delta Company set up its command post inside the perimeter. Distant explosions continued to rock the city, but we were safely out of range.

Me on the left, standing with Sgt. 1st Class Steve Croom in Baghdad.

Having dinner at Ammar's family's house in Baghdad during the lull between the invasion and the insurgency. Clockwise from left: Ammar, Spc. Brandon Moose, Mohamed, Pfc. Eric Poling, Spc. Trent Wykoff, and Pvt. James Worley.

The peppered Volkswagen Passat from which the insurgents tried and failed to launch their attack.

Bravo Company's 3rd Platoon failed miserably in their attempts at covert action. Though garbed in dishdashas, they were pegged immediately as Americans and photographed. Comedians from left, Spc. Adam Sines, Lt. Jim W., and Spc. Zachary Wyant. *Photo courtesy J.W.*

7

Hillah, Iraq
April 2003

The familiar thud of a bomb detonating had been unmistakable—as had the sound of fighter jets off in the distance. The morning was hazy and humid as I sat in the front seat of my truck, listening to a Matchbox 20 song on the satellite radio and eating a warm peach cobbler. We had left the desert, moving around Najaf, and were now within eight miles of the ruins of Babylon. I put the brown plastic spoon back into my snack and looked at it. One package of peaches, two large crackers, four packets of sugar, two packets of cream, some extra water, and a water-activated MRE heater—dessert. I had learned the recipe from Sergeant Croom somewhere between Kuwait and here. Just then I heard another explosion off to the east, but this one sounded *different*. Swallowing some of the cobbler, I figured it was probably a mortar.

The afternoon prior we had inched ever closer to the fighting. Before stopping, we came to within two miles of the

Euphrates River. It surprised me that the Fertile Crescent would begin and end so abruptly. We had been on a desert highway, and after a right turn, had entered into an area full of ditches, tall green grass, and huge palm trees. I could smell the water.

Ancient Babylon is now called Hillah. Sitting along the banks of what is now a Euphrates offshoot, it is a site that has been continuously inhabited for over four thousand years. It has been conquered, liberated, and conquered again. It has been ruled by men known worldwide—men with names like Sargon, Hammurabi, and Nebuchadnezzar.

When we arrived on the outskirts of the town that day, Hillah was the last major Shia city still under the control of Saddam and the Baath Party. The Shias of Hillah had despised him from the very beginning of his reign. They rose against him and had been massacred following the first Gulf War in 1991, their bodies being stacked in graves on the outskirts of the city.

Pushing to within six miles of the city that day, we were reassigned from the ACP back to Delta Company for the attack that was to go off the next morning. I learned this from my commander, Captain Corey B.*, a red-haired West Pointer who had served with the 1st Ranger Battalion before joining the Rakkasans.

The main assault would be two-pronged, from the northwest and from the south. We would attack from the main road leading into Hillah from the west at dawn. In the meantime, a kind of skirmishing force had been sent forward to probe the outskirts of Hillah and to clear all the obstacles in the road.

* Name abbreviated for security purposes.

By midafternoon, the units that had moved forward were in contact. Their brazen move to take down the Iraqi obstacles was too much for the Iraqi defenders to handle. It was an assault on the defenders' pride, and they had chosen confrontation. Events were already unfolding as I dialed into the brigade net, 101.3 WRAK, All Rakkasans, All the Time.

Two Iraqis were already KIA. Two soldiers from Alpha Company had also been wounded, as had one soldier from our company. The Voice said that it was the soldier from Delta who had been the most severely wounded. A piece of shrapnel from an exploding hand grenade had hit him in the face.

I recognized the brigade commander giving instructions. There was talk of maneuvering to take a building, of firing tank rounds into buildings. It was surreal. It was like listening to a game on the radio. *He goes into the shotgun . . . he drops back . . .*

I stuck my head out of the truck to see if I could hear any of the fighting. Nothing. Just a light breeze in the grass and a few voices in the truck parked next to me. I looked up and saw a few wispy clouds and a handful of flying birds. I couldn't hear any of the telltale sounds of combat—no thuds or pop-pop-pops. I guessed that we were still too far away to hear small arms fire. Around me, most guys in the company were just milling about, either bullshitting or lounging in their vehicles. They didn't seem to care that a battle was unfolding six miles away. They didn't seem to care that come morning, it would be us.

I wasn't any different. As if I had no personal stake in the affair, I felt just as interested as if I had been listening to an embedded reporter on CNN back home. *Wow, look honey. Those soldiers are in a fight on TV. What's for dinner?*

For a guy with friends in the line of fire *at that very moment*, I managed to surprise even myself. I hadn't yet realized just how desensitized I was becoming.

By late afternoon the fighting was over. That evening a guy I knew gave me the rundown. He told of an Iraqi who feigned surrender, and then of the Iraqi's comrades who appeared on a flank and began throwing hand grenades. He had ordered his platoon to launch high-explosive grenades from a Mk 19 into each window of a multistory building from which they had taken fire. He told of picking up the shell casings of rounds he had fired. He was keeping them as souvenirs.

By nightfall my detachment had become even creepier by normal standards. The orders had been given, maps had been laminated and disseminated, and the vehicles had been aligned for the morning attack. I had spent an hour trying to get a map of Hillah from the intelligence guys, and then another hour leaning over the hood of my truck in the dark trying to use a permanent marker to properly mark all of the objectives on the map.

I was sitting in the front seat again, listening to music, when Phil, my roommate from back in the States, walked over to me. To Lieutenant Philip Dickinson, another Delta platoon leader, the idea of charging into battle was even newer than it was to me. He had been in Afghanistan with us, but had arrived as a replacement, two days after Anaconda.

It is a chill and dusty morning outside the tents at Kandahar International Airport, and we are shaving out of canteen cups filled with cold water. I've yet to put on my desert camouflage top when I notice a band of new guys have entered our encampment. The first thing that strikes me is how fresh they look, with their pressed uniforms and spotless baggage. Captain K. still has shaving cream on his face when Phil introduces himself as the new officer. Captain K. grunts something and points the clueless-looking new platoon leader over to me. As he walks over, I stick out my hand and say, "How's it going?"

I turned the music down when Phil leaned in, his arm resting on the hood of my truck. I looked up and greeted him. "Sup, dude?"

"Well," he started, "I guess we're ready to go. Everything's lined up."

Lips pursed and eyebrows raised, I nodded under the glow of my hanging green flashlight.

Then he continued. "You know, dude . . . tomorrow is ahh . . . tomorrow's a pretty big day for us."

I grinned up at him. There was no talk of getting killed or maimed or fixing bayonets to go building to building. There was no talk of failure. It was just going to be another day. A big day.

"Yeah," I replied. "Yeah it is." Then I asked him if he was nervous at all.

"You know, I can't say that I am," he said. "Maybe anxious to get going, but I'm not really scared. I guess maybe I should be. I don't know."

I knew what he was talking about. I was headed into urban combat in less than four hours and I wasn't even scared. It was like the moment just before the helicopter touched down on the mountainside during Anaconda.

I was neither happy, sad, scared, nor angry. I don't even remember thinking of my family. I just remember the music before Phil walked over. I didn't think of my parents or my brother or Nikki. There was only the music.

I used it to dull my senses that night, but I knew that in reality I was hooked up to a low-dose adrenaline drip. I was becoming numb. I was becoming a thinking husk with a gun.

When I had eventually called in mortar strikes on non-American targets in the Shah-e-Kot Valley there had been no fear, no anger, no glee. I was a cyborg on a ridgeline putting steel on target. *"Left 100, drop 50. Shot, over . . . Shot, out. Splash, over . . . Splash, out."*

Calling in the strikes became like ordering a pizza. You place an order over the radio for what you want—the type of ordnance you want used, where you want it to land, how much of it you want. "Yes, I'll have four high-explosive mortars on such and such a building in the valley, please. Oh, and can I get two white phosphorous rounds also?" The Voice comes back with something like, "Of course, sir. Would you like smoke rounds with that? Or anything to drink?"

It's times like that, I figure, and times like the fast-approaching morning in Hillah that you become emotionally dead. It is adrenaline. Overdose. Addiction. Your personal weapon becomes the needle, and every time you charge the handle to lock and load before a mission, you inject the adrenaline, which over time will become like heroin to you. You let yourself drift into an emotional coma. If you didn't, you would go mad.

With just over two hours until the attack, Phil left me to my music and my thoughts. I started thinking about my grandfather. He was short and of a slight build, but he was one of the meanest people I'd ever met growing up. He had also been a marine sergeant in the infantry in the Pacific theater during World War II. As he'd gotten older, he'd mellowed out a bit and started carrying around a pocketful of peppermints to hand out to people he liked, but he never lost the edge the Marine Corps had given him. Before I'd received my commission, he'd bought a marine dress uniform so that he could render me my first salute as an officer during the ceremony. Everybody had talked about how cute the old man looked in a dress uniform with tattered ribbons from World War II.

Sitting there listening to the music on low volume, I remembered how before the commissioning, I figured that he'd be impressed when I told him that I too had joined the infantry. To my surprise, he'd just kind of shrugged and shaken his head. A year and a half later, over conversation about my experience in Afghanistan, he'd looked at my grandmother quizzically and said, "I never understood why the boy went and joined the infantry." He said this as if I weren't standing there next to them listening. Now, in my current predicament—about to head off into combat again—I wished that I could have talked to him. I would have said, "Okay. Now I get it."

I was just about to doze off when I had the sudden urge to take a shit. For a second I thought I would just hold it, but then I remembered that sometimes, urban combat could drag on for days. I figured I'd better take care of it now and worry about sleeping later. I knew I probably wouldn't really sleep anyway.

As I stepped out of the truck to grab my shovel and head off into the night, I noticed some guys from the company kneeling in the darkness in prayer circles. I thought that it must be nice to have something like that on which to lean when headed into a possible shitstorm. It must be quite calming to know that by praying hard, God will be rooting for your side. Walking past them I thought about the character Ceranno in the baseball movie *Major League,* when he is discussing the link between divine help and hitting breaking pitches. "Ahh, Hay-seuss," the big Latin American ballplayer says, "I laak him vera much. But he no help with curveball."

Or with RPGs and small arms fire.

Captain K. has ordered me to go up on the high ground overlooking the valley to call in mortar strikes on suspected al Qaeda positions.

As I make my way up the rocky incline covered in dried yellow grass, I notice that Sam Edwards and some of his guys are already up there, watching. When I reach the top, I can't help but stand there and stare out at the decimated villages below. My eyes are transfixed, just as they had been during the bombing of a few nights earlier. This is the closest I have come to the valley in daylight. It's still half a mile away, but I feel as though I could reach out and touch some of the mud-brick buildings. It's a battlefield, and I'm captivated by it. Sam sees me.

"Hey, man! Get down! Shit!"

I look at him resting on a knee several feet away from me. He looks strained, even older than I remember him being just a few days ago. It makes me realize what I'm doing. I'm standing there, in the wide open with no trees or vegetation for concealment. I'm a lone figure standing on an overlook, against the backdrop of nothing but blue sky. And I'm about to draw fire from the valley if I don't change that quickly.

I duck and take a knee. Sam then tells me where the terrorists are suspected of hiding. He has already called in several strikes, so he knows. There is an al Qaeda anti-aircraft gun on Takhur Gar that I have in mind. We've been listening to it fire intermittently for two days, and thus far, no one has been able to disable it. But from our vantage point we can only hit the valley.

I grasp the hand mike from the radio and take another look at the landscape below. For the first time I see a brown horse, standing alone in a corral on the valley floor. For two days I've heard about this horse—through word of mouth and even once or twice on the radio. As I look down into the valley, it is the first thing to which my eye is drawn. The horse stands in stark contrast to everything around it.

The villages are now mostly rubble—cratered and blackened. I see firsthand what this horse has had to endure with each successive barrage of carpet-bombing, mortars, snipers, and helicopter attacks. I've also come to understand that people have been trying to kill it with a sense of passive cruelty. No overt efforts—just a sniper round here, a mortar there. They've yet to succeed, however. From my vantage point I can see that the horse is the only living thing in the valley, the only thing still moving in the open. It starts to trot to the other side of the corral, bucking its head once as it prances. It looks to be enjoying the warm sun along with the brief respite in the shooting. I try to comprehend how it has managed to make it this far—standing alone in the crossfire of this no-man's land.

One of Sam's soldiers sees me watching it. "Hey sir, you gonna try to hit the horse with the mortars?"

Without looking at him I say, "No, I'm going to try to hit the terrorists."

"Aw, come on, sir. You can't hit them . . . well, you can't see 'em at least, even if you do hit 'em. Wouldn't it be cooler to hit the horse?"

I turn my head and glare at him, deadpan. I turn my head back to the valley and put the hand mike up to my mouth. "Bulldog 9-5, this is 1-6, adjust fire, polar, over."

"This is Bulldog 9-5, adjust fire, polar, out."

"Roger, direction 4-520, distance 1-1-0-0. . . ."

* * *

In under a minute, explosive projectiles that I have ordered like a grande mocha cappuccino at Starbucks are careening over my head toward human beings, hunkered down in dug out fighting positions. They also fly in the direction of a single brown horse—a horse that's probably wondering what it has done to deserve this.

By late afternoon the weather has started to roll into the Shah-e-Kot Valley. I walk up onto a different piece of high ground with Sergeant Collins where we stand with Takhur Gar looming over us, watching the storm approach in the distance. We watch it travel from west to east, first enveloping the ridge known as the "Whale," and then slowly moving across the open valley.

As the sunlight fades, we begin preparing for nightfall. The forecast is calling for a low around fifteen degrees—coupled with a wind chill that could drop well below zero. I try to remember if I've ever been that cold before.

By dusk it is snowing on our own ridgeline. It starts with big, fat flakes, before turning to the more plentiful small ones. It snows without respite for the duration of the night. The guys on watch have it the worst—they have to sit up on the high ground with no cover against the wind. Those of us in the low ground fare little better, with no shelter and few sleeping bags.

For the first part of the night I stay awake pondering life and listening to the sound of my teeth chattering. I gaze at the stars and listen to sporadic gunfire and accompanying explosions, all the while wishing I could be somewhere else. I wonder about the horse.

Around three in the morning, with teeth working like little off-white jackhammers, I give up on trying to rest. I start pacing in small circles on the rocky, snow-covered, and now muddy ground. I notice that this has become the first quiet night of the operation. There is no crackle of machine-gun fire in the distance; there is no Spectre gunship on station searching for enemy positions with its infrared beam. All has gone silent in the snowfall.

A few minutes later Sergeant Pascoe joins me. He is doing the same thing. It is simply too cold to sleep or even to sit still. We stand there conversing in whispers until the sky begins to lighten. We talk for several hours, though now I can't recall a word that was said.

We are technically in combat, but in reality we are just two shivering guys standing on a mountain, talking about life and wondering if it will end soon.

The darkness was an inky black when I lifted my head up. I had been dozing in the front seat of my truck, half sitting and half leaning to my left on the console. I had used my load-bearing vest with its canteens and ammo magazines as a pillow. Looking out the front windshield I could make out the faint glows of several flashlights with red, green, and blue filters. I glanced at my watch. Not quite 4 a.m.

The plan was for the artillery to fire on targets in Hillah while we were still on the outskirts of town. Once that was done, the tanks would move forward with the dismounted infantry following on trucks. Then, inside this city of over 300,000 people, the Delta platoons, mine included, would be used to seize and secure key traffic intersections while the tanks drove forward into the heart of Hillah. Apache helicopters would be waiting on the east side of Hillah, hovering. Their mission was to destroy any Iraqi regular or irregular force that might attempt to flee what I thought, by that point, could be a burning city.

By 4:30 I had checked and rechecked our preparations with Sergeant Croom and my two section leaders, Sergeants Alex

Estrada and Michael Whipple. With fifteen minutes to go, I sat
in the darkness pondering the idea that we could be driving
into a hornet's nest—pondering the idea that I might never see
another sunrise.

Through the darkness I could barely make out the silhou-
ettes of the trucks and tanks in the formation. I could hear
them, however. Every vehicle in the convoy had been idling for
minutes. The entire battalion sounded alive, as if it were a single organism—a lurking predator about to pounce. Outside the
din of rumbling around me I could hear the jetlike whine of
the tanks further ahead. The length of the column was such
that it snaked around groves of palm trees and through the
grassy field.

Radio traffic on the Delta Company net had been high as
the platoons conducted final checks and procedures.
Suddenly I heard the voice of Captain B.'s driver and RTO
come across the airwaves. Corporal Davis announced that
the lead vehicles, that being the tanks, were now beginning
their advance toward Hillah. I keyed my hand mike on the
platoon net and passed on the message to my other five
humvees. I looked at my watch, pushed the Indiglo button,
and saw that it was 4:45 a.m. I thought briefly about the
defenders of Al Hillah and wondered what they would decide
to do. Regardless, their time was up.

My driver, Sergeant Thomas Hemingson, steered onto the
main road and we began following Estrada's vehicle. Alejandro
"Alex" Estrada was the informal point man in the platoon. He
was short, stocky, and like everyone else, his dark hair had been
shaved bald. He was the type of section sergeant that Croom
and I could leave alone to just do his thing. He was dependable.

The convoy started moving at a steady fifteen miles an hour beneath the morning stars. As we drove, houses and buildings began to appear on both sides of the road. In one window I saw the silhouette of a person in front of what looked to be candlelight.

I wondered what they must have been thinking as they watched this rumbling column move through their neighborhood. With no streetlights, they had no way of clearly seeing us. They could only peek through window shades and listen. It was loud to be sure, but there was no shooting or yelling, there was no honking or screeching of tires. None of the preconceptions I had associated with an attack on a major city were being met. We were driving calmly and steadily in murky blackness.

When we made our final pause before the assault, light was beginning to filter in through the palm trees and the humid haze surrounding us. I looked down at my map. By the length of the column I presumed that the tanks in front had to be stopped at the "Welcome to Hillah" sign I supposed was somewhere up ahead. I also became aware that to my right, in a patch of low ground off the side of the road, was a battery of howitzer artillery pieces. I could see the American soldiers that manned them moving around, readying them to initiate the attack.

As we sat there in the middle of the road, artillery prepping to fire, a man dressed in a suit and carrying a briefcase walked out of what looked to be his home. I could see that he had a moustache and that his black hair was balding on top. He took the sidewalk on the left side of the street and began walking toward Hillah, his briefcase swaying as he went. As I watched this, I observed that he never once looked at the armored column parked not thirty yards away from him. He just kept walking toward Hillah. Like he was going to work.

I didn't know who was crazier, him or us. But it struck me that, of the two of us, he was the one taking part in the more natural act.

As the man disappeared into the distance ahead, I noticed a couple of dogs running around. And a chicken. Then I heard the voice of Corporal Davis come over the company net. He announced that the artillery was about to fire. After that, he said, the head of the column would initiate the attack run into the center of Hillah.

I looked down into the low ground. The moving artillery soldiers were too far away for me to hear anything. To me, they looked small and silent. I could hear all of our vehicle engines running, but no one spoke. There was radio silence for the first time that morning. I looked again into the low ground. This time even the artillerymen were still.

And then without further warning, the attack began. I nearly came out of my seat when it did. I knew it was coming, but I had no idea that it would be as loud as it was. A full two hundred yards away, the cannon fire seemed to be emanating from inside my own head.

They quickly reloaded and went back to pulling lanyards. The roar was deafening. This time there were bright muzzle flashes. Twice more they fired, sending high-explosive shells careening into the city.

Suddenly I felt different—as if the artillery pieces had awakened me along with the rest of Hillah. The numbness metamorphosed again, this time into a kind of confident, frenzied, euphoria. Adrenaline reserves were being released into every cell in my body. The levees had broken. There was no fear. There wasn't even any danger. Nothing was going to stand in the way of this armored onslaught. I had a vision of us slicing into the heart of Babylon, the horrified enemy fleeing before us.

For the first time in combat I felt invincible. I could sense the fear of those in Hillah—and I was feeding off of it. There was blood in the water.

The lead tanks began entering the city.

Pressing into the city, my left hand cradled the radio's hand mike up to my left ear, while my right hand held my M4, balanced on the windowsill and pointed out. With no warning a Kiowa helicopter flew directly over the top of my truck. It was less than a hundred feet off the ground and headed toward the front of the attacking column. Now looking at the sky, I caught a glimpse of another one to my right, just before I lost it behind a building. The small but maneuverable birds had timed their appearance to coincide perfectly with the entrance of the tanks into the city.

The buildings we passed were generally low and grimy. There were a few apartment buildings with clotheslines strung across the balconies, some of which were adorned with freshly cleaned clothes. As we closed on our first phase line, I quickly became aware of two things on which I hadn't planned.

The first was the speed with which we were pressing forward—and the lack of resistance that came with it. I looked down at the map and saw that we were rapidly closing on Objective Wolf, one of the widest four-way intersections in

Hillah. I surmised that the lead of the formation must already be there. This was interesting because Wolf was already halfway to the center of town and I'd yet to take any fire, and I'd heard nothing on the radio of anyone else being in contact either.

While it appeared that no one wanted to tangle with us, the opposite was true for simple observation. With each block gobbled up in our drive, more and more people started coming out of their houses. They began to line the streets.

At first they showed no emotion—there were no smiles and waves. Several blocks later it changed. Suddenly a man on the right side of the road raised his fist. My hackles went up and I glared at him. With my weapon pointed in his direction, my right index finger moved gently onto the trigger. But then I saw that he was waving the fist not in anger, but in triumph. As I passed him, I saw the look I had mistaken for rage. It was a look of vindication.

Then I heard a whistle. To my left I saw a younger man with a goatee clapping. I turned to Sergeant Hemingson in the driver's seat and said, "Are you seeing this?"

With the tanks plowing into the center of Hillah like arctic icebreakers, Corporal Davis abruptly stopped my platoon with a message over the radio.

We had just driven through a traffic light and entered Objective Wolf. It had begun to fill with people when Davis called me. He had instructions that my platoon was to stop and hold the objective until the entire battalion had passed through it. Then we were to hold the position and prevent anyone from circling in behind the column.

I relayed the message to Croom and the section leaders. Whipple swung his truck around, while the commander of the other truck in his section followed. Croom and I stayed with Sergeant Estrada's section, where we took up positions to the south and east. I stepped out just in time to see Sergeant Croom parking right behind me. I quickly scanned the intersection. The gunners were staying in the vehicles manning their weapons while the drivers were standing outside of the trucks, still holding the fully stretched radio hand mikes. The four truck commanders were standing beside the trucks as well, monitoring the growing crowd and scanning for snipers. The sun was just beginning to peek from behind the buildings to the east. It was going to be a spotless blue-sky day.

The first sound I noticed was the distinctive crackle of gunfire. It wasn't aimed at us, so I looked for other things with which to concern myself. I looked back to the western end of the intersection and saw a large building. The entire face of one side had a painting of Saddam Hussein in all his grandeur. He was wearing a hat and his arm was outstretched. I thought that it looked kind of ironic, considering the fact that his arm was outstretched in the direction of an American heavy weapons platoon.

As I was gazing up at Saddam, a Kiowa helicopter sped low and fast across the northern end of the intersection. With it came a hail of gunfire. Sergeant Croom hustled over to me and exclaimed, "You see that? They're shootin' at the bird!"

"Yep," I said with an eyebrow raise. Standing a few feet away from my truck, I started inching closer to it. For the first time I was having second thoughts about only having one AK-47-proof plate in my vest. The Defense Department had seen to it that we only had enough front and back plates for our gunners before the invasion. I noticed Sergeant Croom backing up against my truck as well.

Above the din of the crowd I could hear a helicopter coming closer. For a brief moment my mind slipped back into the mountains, and I fully expected to see an Apache or a Cobra fly over a snow-covered ridge.

Lying flat on the high ground, I watch as the first Apache streaks down the valley from north to south, while the second breaks off to the right and flies toward the Whale. Seconds later, two Marine Corps Super Cobras follow. The four helicopters begin scanning for al Qaeda positions. Within seconds the shooting starts.

It is a one-sided fight. The attack helicopters are able to strike with impunity now that the American infantry has pinned down the terrorists—and they do. Each bird circles around an area and then hovers, as if looking at something. Then it circles around again. Finally it sees something—a person or movement—worth engaging. The resulting fusillade of rockets and 40mm gunfire is devastating. Dust and debris is thrown up with each strike, the rattle of the chain guns echoing through the crisp air. For what seems like an hour, the birds loiter over the expanse of the Shah-e-Kot Valley, mauling anything that moves and some things that don't.

Again, as they had two days earlier, the Apaches look animate to me. At Bagram they had looked beaten down, but now they now look enraged. They appear to me as sentient beings on a mission of retribution for their wounded comrades. Each time one of them wheels and turns to face a target, it looks personal—as if these machine-like beings with homunculi for pilots can somehow exude anger.

In the middle of Hillah, no Apache came. Instead, it was the same Kiowa that sped across the northern edge of the intersection.

Again, gunfire erupted behind the building directly to our north, following the bird as it zipped between buildings.

In combat you learn very quickly to differentiate between "gunfire that concerns you," "gunfire that doesn't concern you," and "gunfire that should be monitored." Nobody outside of the military realizes this, but you can be on a battlefield, explosions and shooting all around, and find yourself walking around without your helmet, eating an MRE, or discussing the merits of one sexual position over another. This is because you're surrounded by "gunfire that doesn't concern you." On the other hand, when it does concern you, you're usually very aware of this fact. The fire coming from behind the building, we silently agreed with a head nod, was "gunfire that should be monitored."

As I listened to the cacophony of noises—people, helicopters, and gunfire—I began scrutinizing the throng of onlookers. That's when Sergeant Estrada walked over and told me about the bomb.

"That guy," he said, pointing to a man standing next to his truck, "says there's a bomb in the ditch over there." He pointed to the southeastern corner of the intersection.

I raised my eyebrows and said, "A bomb?"

Estrada said, "Yeah, he says it's in the ditch."

I followed Estrada as he led me to the informant. After an awkward introduction I asked him about the bomb. We were standing within fifty feet of the area in question.

The Iraqi looked at me, shrugged, and said, "Yes . . . over there. In the hole in the ground." He said it with a total lack of gravity attached to his statement—as if this were normal.

You know, just like the rest of the bombs in holes in the ground.

I said, "Okay, hold on. Let me see what I can do." What I wanted to do was pick up my platoon and head far, far away. We had been stationary for much too long. At this point, having never before captured a city, held an intersection, or dealt with civilians on a battlefield, I was starting to get a little *edgy*. This was more up close and personal than anything I'd ever done in Afghanistan, and I was currently watching helicopters getting shot at. I opened the door to my humvee and got in. I picked up the hand mike to the company net and keyed it. I was feeling complacent and exposed.

Davis answered.

"Roger, there's a guy here that says there's a bomb in a ditch here on Objective Wolf. Any word on how long they want us to hold this thing? Over."

"A bomb? Did you see it?"

"Negative, over."

Davis paused. "Stand by."

After a few seconds he came back. "3-6, Six says he wants you to go see what it is, over."

I stifled a laugh. "No way, over." I keyed the hand mike again before Davis could respond. I realized that I had just refused a lawful order over the company net. "Six Romeo, this is 3-6, I, uhh, just don't think that would be a very good idea right now based on the current situation," I said, softening my tone. "I, uhh, we don't really know what we're doing, over."

"Roger, stand by," he answered. For thirty long seconds I waited, expecting a firm rebuke. Eventually Davis replied. "3-6, Six says you can leave it alone, over."

I let out a breath. Then I heard Davis again.

"3-6, Six says you're to pick up your platoon and move from Objective Wolf to the bus station. The lead element is about to cross the river onto Objective Weasel, over."

"Roger," I said, letting out a sigh of relief.

When we arrived downtown, half the battalion was clogged at an intersection. They were waiting for the tanks to cross the Shatt al Hillah, the Euphrates offshoot around which Hillah is built. Sergeant Collins and Bravo Company were in the midst of clearing the bridge. Meanwhile, most of Delta Company was holding the intersection near the bridge.

As the sun had gotten higher, the day had gotten hazy again. We were in an oddly shaped four-way intersection that backed up to the river. In front of me was a dust-colored, four-story building with a white billboard sign atop it. The sign said "Konika" in large red letters and in both English and Arabic. Next to my idling humvee was an eight-foot high concrete frame. Inside it was a canvas painting of Saddam Hussein from the waist up. He was grinning and wearing a suit.

The crowd had been kept at bay so far, but they were quickly starting to encroach on our intersection, just as they had on Objective Wolf. I gathered from the current radio chatter that nearly all the units attacking concurrently were meeting minimal resistance. Looking at my map with all its objectives and phase lines, the significance of that occurred to me. The thought was this: *Once we cross the river and establish a bridgehead on the other side, this thing will be over. The city will be completely under our control.*

The resistance had melted away apparently—vanishing into the honeycombed buildings and palm forests around the city. The Republican Guard was gone. The Fedayeen, too. Even the guy shooting at the Kiowa had disappeared.

No one had expected anything like this to happen. They had just quit. They had relinquished Babylon. And the people knew it too. The swell of onlookers began getting louder and more cheerful about the situation. It was as if none of us knew what to do. In our moment of victory over the Baath Party we were confused, and the Iraqis seemed to be as well. The sudden change in circumstances caught everyone off guard. No one knew whether to celebrate or to continue bracing for explosions. No one knew who was in charge anymore. You could hear the vacuum in authority sucking restraint out of the city.

A sergeant in another platoon walked over to the canvas of Saddam. Without hesitating, and in plain view of the citizens of Hillah, he reached up and tore it down. He quickly folded it up, put it under his arm, and carried it back to his humvee. His face was defiant, his expression read: *That's right, motherfuckers. I did it.* For an instant I felt awkward, unsure of whether or not we could do that. I didn't know my role. This was the first time I had ever actually *conquered* some place. I had *vanquished* people in the past, but I'd never *conquered* anyone.

It was then that I realized we could do whatever we wanted to do. Images of Saddam in Iraq were sacrosanct, and they were everywhere. They were the watchful eyes that looked over all of Iraq. They were symbolic of all that was powerful in a land ruled by brute force. And they were things you didn't fuck with unless you wanted your family killed. For me, and for those who saw him do it, it was a split-second in which you could sense that tide turning irreversibly.

Several hours later we were inside the gates of an Iraqi Army base on the north side of Hillah. Outside the compound were thousands of celebrating Iraqis. In the time since the canvas had been ripped down, all of Hillah had come out, dancing in the streets. The first chance I got, I dialed in CNN on the radio. I was expecting to hear something of our victorious takeover in Hillah.

Instead I learned that American troops were presently in the center of Baghdad. At that very moment they were in the process of pulling down a statue of Saddam in Firdaws Square. I called out to our chaplain, who happened to be the person nearest to me at the time. "Hey!" I waved to him. "Come over here and listen to this!"

He walked over and stuck his head into the open door of my humvee. Together, we listened, neither moving nor speaking. After a while the chaplain looked up at me with an expression that combined incredulity, skepticism, and astonishment all in the same glance. He said, "I mean . . . I guess . . . I mean, it's over."

The sense of relief that came washing over us was palpable. Five minutes earlier we had been prepared for a bloody siege of Baghdad, for violent urban warfare. Now I was thinking that I could be home within six weeks. I was conscious of the feeling that now I knew I wasn't going to die. When I heard of the statue falling in Baghdad, fifty miles away, the weight of considering my own death had fallen away with it. Silently euphoric, I sat there in the front seat of my humvee. I was covered in dirt and sweat, but I was in the shade, and the radio had been switched back to music.

At dusk I took my platoon back into the center of the city. The Iraqis of Hillah were shooting guns, honking horns, and defacing everything that bore an image of Saddam.

We were traveling south on one of Hillah's main avenues and traffic was tight. Everybody who had a car was out driving around and celebrating. For me though, it wasn't personal. I was too strung out emotionally to feel anything. I had taken part in the storming of the city like a robot and I would leave the city, I assumed, in the same fashion, intent on mopping up Baghdad in similar fashion.

And that's when the white four-door car in the right hand lane nearly crashed into my truck, causing me to put my thoughts on hold. I yelled at Sergeant Hemingson, "Hey, look out . . . car! Fuck!"

The white car swerved right, putting a few feet between our two moving vehicles. I thought he might be trying to ram us. Then the driver swung his car back in my direction. My index finger drifted to the safety switch on my M4.

As he pulled within three feet of my speeding humvee, I stared, wide-eyed, at the driver. He was an Iraqi man probably in his forties or early fifties. He had a thick, dark moustache with hair to match. However, his hair had receded on top, leaving most of his head completely bald. I looked at his eyes, hoping to glean from them his intentions.

Keeping both hands on the wheel, he was nodding his head backward, pointing with his eyes toward the back seat. I could see that he was smiling. I was confused. Slowly I took my gaze from his face and moved it along the car toward the rear window of the moving car. I expected to see some form of weaponry pointed at me.

Instead, I saw a little girl of no more than five wearing a white dress. She was outstretched, leaning half of her small body out of the car's backseat window. Her arm was fully extended. In her tiny hand she held a rose.

Then things became clear. I said, "Hey man, get closer."

"What?" Hemingson asked incredulously.

"Just do it," I said, shifting my gun to my other hand. "Slow down and get closer."

When he did, I stretched out my arm in its desert camouflage sleeve, reaching for the little girl. A moment later I grasped the stemless rose, briefly touching her hand. With the flower now in my possession, I withdrew my arm. She smiled at me. For a brief second I smiled back. As we began to pull away from the white car I glanced back at the man driving. Still smiling, he simply nodded at me.

Shivering in the cold on the roof of an Iraqi barracks building that night, I was at the same time relieved and let down. I suddenly saw the attack on Hillah as being a big cock-tease. I had gotten so mentally prepared for bullets ricocheting off walls and RPGs crisscrossing in front of me that I couldn't let it go. Now that the danger was over, I had reverted to being a junkie who needed a fix. I was jealous of the 3rd Infantry Division in Baghdad—they were getting action and I was desperate for some. As I saw it, I had now been in two wars and never squeezed the trigger on my own personal weapon. I had combat blue-balls.

I was a raving storm trooper, but I was humiliatingly petri-fied of death. I wanted to fight, but I didn't want to hurt any-body. I wanted to be a hero and I didn't care if I was hero. I felt alive inside, but disconnected from everyone. I loved my family and friends and I didn't care if I ever saw them again.

I was suffering from emotional whiplash.

8

Baghdad
April 2003

As we approached the city limit, the first thought in my head on seeing the city was, *Yep. That's what it looked like on TV.* It was a city alight with red tracers—tracers that glowed white in our green night vision. Some slashed horizontally through the darkness, while others arced upward into the night sky. But now they weren't originating from the well-known anti-aircraft guns positioned throughout the city. Now the fight was close—now the tracers were from machine guns, Bradleys, and AK-47s.

I knew so little of Baghdad before I first entered it, that now, looking back, I don't see how I could have been so ignorant. When we left Hillah, all I knew of the Iraqi capital was what I had seen on TV in the first Gulf War—it was green and black at night there, and they had lots of anti-air-craft guns. That was what I knew. However, when I thought of the *idea* of Baghdad, my mind conjured other images—magic lamps and flying carpets; Ali Baba and Aladdin;

Scheherazade and Sinbad. When we finally entered the city, half of me expected to be met by bullets and anarchy, the other half by cartoon characters.

We swept into Baghdad on a night that found the city's resistance in its final hours. The airport had been seized, the statue of Saddam toppled, and the Marines were thrusting into the eastern portion of the city. We entered from the south, on an abandoned Highway Eight. We were streaking down the empty road, looking for the interchange with the Daura Expressway. I hadn't been prepared for the sheer size of Baghdad, for its freeways, loops, and exits.

My section and squad leaders started calling about the tracer fire. "3-6, this 3-3, we've got tracer fire off to the left, four hundred meters, over."

"3-6, this is 3-1, 3-2 says he saw some fire off to the right, two separate bursts, over."

They kept coming.

"3-6, this is 3-4, I just saw a tracer to my left, four hundred meters, over."

I liked the fact that they were alert, but this was definitely "gunfire that didn't concern us." Nothing was coming our way. I got back on the radio.

"Hey, listen up," I said. "We're clogging the net with all these reports. I know you guys see tracer fire. *We're in the middle of a battle.*" The italics were verbal and blatant. "That's what you're *supposed* to be seeing. This is *normal* for these conditions." I wanted to say, "Call me if you *stop* seeing tracers. That's something I need to know. That will be newsworthy."

Sergeant Croom cut in. "3-6, don't you think they need to report this stuff? It's kinda important, over."

I thought about it for a second. For once I actually felt like I was correct in the midst of dissent from all the NCOs in the platoon. "No," I stated flatly. "I need to know when the fire is directed at *you*."

That night we escaped attention and camped out under the stars in a farmer's field, surrounded by a forest of palms.

The Daura refinery is the main oil processing point in Baghdad. Its towering and flaming stacks are symbols of the city's vitality—when they are snuffed out, the city goes with them. In the first Gulf War, Allied planes had bombed the refinery, rendering it useless for nearly a year. This time, however, the refinery—the economic heart of the city—was spared from destruction. It sat against a bend in the Tigris River, between the river and the Daura Expressway. Before dawn we finalized plans to clear an eight-square-mile area of which the refinery sat directly in the center.

The battalion didn't really have a mission in the strictest sense of the word. Instead we were tasked with "clearing" the area. The word "clear" in this case was used very loosely and very subjectively. It basically meant that we were to use the forces of order and goodness to neutralize the forces of chaos and evil. That could mean anything from attacking foreign fighters to stopping looters to capturing weapons caches to observing traffic patterns. There was no plan. There were only sectors. This is your sector. Go there and clear it.

So Sergeant Croom and I, along with our fourteen soldiers, set off into the urban wilderness of Baghdad. We had six humvees, lots of ammunition, over a million dollars worth of equipment, and no idea what the fuck we were going to do with it all.

After its sacking during the Mongol invasion, Baghdad never fully recovered its previous economic or cultural prominence. To that point, the city had been the flourishing center of the classical Islamic world with a population of up to a million people. When Hulagu Khan led the Mongols in their attack on the city in 1258, they slaughtered eight hundred thousand of the city's inhabitants. They also destroyed the city's irrigation system—a move that effectively ended the Abbasid Caliphate. Afterward, the city that had been a major hub of commerce on the road to China shrunk to just over a hundred thousand people. From the time of the Khan's invasion, Baghdad has gradually rebuilt itself, literally from the ground up—suffering through other, less drastic occupations all along the way.

When we arrived on that April morning as the latest in this long string of invading armies, the city had nearly six million residents and a Western-style urban infrastructure. Several of the six million made our first few hours interesting with some periodic harassing fire. They would fire one round and take off, making me even more jumpy than I already was.

An abandoned battery of anti-aircraft artillery sat unattended in a grassy field, just off the Daura Expressway. Croom had radioed me with the information. I asked him if he'd done anything about it and he said no. He said he hadn't felt too keen on the idea of leaving the road to go traipsing around Iraqi Army positions in the open without any cover. When I saw the same pieces from the road I didn't have to think twice about the decision to get out and explore.

I stepped out and shut the door. As I did so, a few of the first Iraqi cars and trucks to venture out that day sped past us, probably curious to get a look. I turned to look in the direction of Sergeant Krueger's truck when the glint of something on the ground next to one of his tires caught my eye.

As I walked over, I could see that it was a pile of discarded clothes. On top of the pile was a shiny object reflecting the morning sun. I picked it up.

It was an Iraqi campaign ribbon with a medal attached. The two-inch-long ribbon was striped in four colors—red, white, green, white again, and then black. The red, white, and green I knew were the colors of the Iraqi flag. The medal itself was an eight-pointed gold star with a solid black circle in the middle. Inside were two swords pointed upward. Above them was a red triangle within which was the Iraqi eagle. The ribbon, I noticed, looked faded and worn. Probably, I thought, thrown in the road by a soldier fearing American retribution. I would learn only later that the ribbon had been issued for service during the Mother of All Battles in 1991.

Estrada and I set out to check the triple-A guns while Krueger stayed on the highway to direct the gunners who were providing cover. The anti-aircraft guns were set two hundred yards off the expressway, in a green field of waist-high grass. We gingerly walked down a slight hill and then picked up a dirt road leading from the highway down the length of the field. On one side of the road was the field; on the other was a thick orchard.

At the same time Captain B. and Corporal Davis, along with Phil Dickinson and some of his guys, were nearer the refinery investigating their own set of artillery pieces. They had discovered theirs around the same time we found ours.

Estrada and I picked up the hard-packed dirt track and began following it. After about a hundred and fifty yards, we came to a tree on the edge of the path. Beneath it were the abandoned belongings of Iraqi soldiers. There were clothes and black leather combat boots. There were three or four yellowish helmets. There were also the remains of what had been a meal. They had left everything and disappeared.

I had never seen an anti-aircraft gun before. The first one we came to was painted the same flat yellow as the helmets. It was sitting on the edge of the dirt road, looking broken and abandoned by owners who had bailed out in a hurry. The barrel was pointed level, as if its caretakers had lowered its aim from the sky in a final act of capitulation. I noticed that the gun was still locked and loaded. Around the artillery piece were strewn over a hundred rounds of ammunition. There were bits of wood and pieces of metal— the remnants of the ammo boxes broken apart to load the weapon.

I picked one of the projectiles up.

"Fifty-seven millimeter, high explosive, sir," Davis explained to Captain B. He was looking down at the forearm-length triple-A round he held in his hands. They all had their hands on the gun, each soldier exploring the still-loaded weapon from a different angle.

Phil stood watching as Captain B. asked if anyone had a clue as to how to unload it. The commander didn't want to leave the artillery unattended while it was still capable of wreaking havoc. Davis set his round down and said, "I bet I can do it. It doesn't look too hard."

He stepped up onto the platform and then sat down in the anti-aircraft gunner's seat.

The large caliber ammunition I held said "57-MM, High Explosive." I didn't like it for some reason, though. Because it was larger, it gave me the irrational feeling that it was more volatile than the grenades I'd been used to carrying. I set it down and then turned to Estrada who was poking around some other pieces of equipment. We made eye contact and then I just shrugged and said, "Huh."

We stepped out onto the dirt road away from the cannon. I had my hands on my hips and I was scanning the whole field, wondering who I should call and how we should handle this. I thought it was a bad idea to leave the pieces out there unattended.

Davis squinted his eyes, searching for the triple-A equivalent of a charging handle. When his hand found something that seemed like it would eject the round, he smiled. Then the corporal looked up at the captain and lieutenant and said, "Oh here, I think you just pull this down . . . ."

The explosion tore through the orchard with a thunderous roar. Estrada and I turned and we ran. We didn't say anything. We didn't even look at each other. We just ran. I began sprinting back down the dirt road. Estrada went another way, darting into the field.

* * *

Captain B., Davis, and Phil watched in wide-eyed horror as the round skipped off the ground like a stone on water, careening into the orchard in front of them and disappearing.

I was running at full speed wearing an armor-plated vest, carrying 210 rounds of ammunition, and an M4. It did not slow me down one bit. My arms were pumping in long sweeping motions, my legs stretching out to grab longer and longer pieces of ground with each stride. I could see the humvees on the road—far, far away.

Estrada was running in a diagonal direction from me. I could see that he was already in the center of the grassy field. The poor guy was running zigzags in a weak effort to make himself a harder target to hit.

As I ran I was convinced that we had just walked into an Iraqi ambush. I was certain that they had just blown a claymore mine and for some reason were delaying the act of opening fire on us. Maybe they were surprised it had missed us.

I began gulping air as my lungs started to burn under the weight of my equipment. As I got closer, I could see Krueger's gunner steadying his aim on the Mk 19, ready to open fire on anything that moved.

By the time I got back to the incline at the edge of the highway my lungs were nearly bursting. Somehow I dragged myself safely back to the trucks. In gasping breaths, I tried to ask Krueger if anyone had seen anything. "Did you . . . did you guys . . . did you see . . ?" I stopped trying to talk and just pointed in the general direction of the Iraqi guns.

The range of normality is expanded in a war zone. After a while, you get so desensitized that big guns can become little guns, and big deals can become not-so-big deals. Like when someone accidentally fires a high explosive round at you from a crew-served anti-aircraft cannon—in the middle of a bustling city, not two hundred yards from an expressway.

When Phil told me later that night what happened, I just thought it was kind of amusing and gave him an eyebrow raise and shrug of the shoulders. By the time Davis had launched the 57mm anti-aircraft round at Estrada and me, I was serene about the fact that, on a battlefield, things tend to go flying where they're not supposed to.

The morning has dawned clear and sunny. For us, nothing has changed. Our mission is still to block and call in mortars—and to await word on whether Zia's Afghan troops will sweep through the valley or not. From what I understand, they are still in Gardez regrouping and recovering. After spending the night staving off frostbite, Zia's indecision is not something about which I want to hear. As usual, Sergeant Collins wants to charge down into the valley, end it, and go home. I have mixed feelings about that, but know that what either of us wants has absolutely no bearing on the situation.

By midmorning half the platoon is actively scanning for movement in the valley, while the other half thaws out in the warm sun. The day's bombs have just begun to fall on Takhur Gar, Terghul Gar, and the valley. After thirty-six hours in the Shah-e-Kot, this is already beginning to feel like a regular day at the office.

For some reason, no matter how much I prepare, I am never ready for the moment when it comes.

This time it is the dreaded whistle—although it actually sounds more like an extended zzzZZZ. It has been the last noise heard by thousands of soldiers around the world for decades. It is the sound of incoming. I look to the sky. I see it falling. It is dark, maybe black. It is fifty feet off the ground. It is falling. It is falling fast. It will land on my platoon. It will not negotiate.

When it impacts, I will no longer exist.

This is it. This is my only thought in the one second before I die. I can't get down before it hits. I am moving in water—in slow motion. I am trying to dive—trying to live. I must get as flat as possible.

It strikes the earth within feet of Private Paguaga. I can't recall hearing the sound that comes with the impact. I am only aware that I am still alive. I start yelling, "Mortars! Mortars! Mortars!" *I hear other voices calling out:* "Incoming! Incoming!" *I am trying to bury my face into the ground and call out orders at the same time.*

We have been targeted. In a matter of seconds the sky will start raining mortars. And we're just sitting here. We're not dug in. We have no cover. And we sure as hell haven't received any warning.

For a second we wait. Everyone is flat on the ground. No one knows what to do—run or hold. We are trained to run—to get out of the impact area—but in this case we have been ordered to hold this ground. Another few seconds pass. Suddenly from ground zero comes a raised arm. It is Private Paguaga. He is still lying flat, but waving his arm for all to see.

"I'm okay!" *he calls out in his thick Nicaraguan accent.* "I'm okay! I'm okay!" *At this point I am struck by the fact that the projectile— whatever it was—had not detonated. It had been a dud. But now we await the rest. I lay there bracing myself.*

The air has become quiet again and the CP is silent as well. They seem just as confused as we are.

Then Taylor summons me to the radio.

Of the select group of humans who have heard the sound of a satellite-guided bomb right before impact, not many have survived to tell the world what the noise is. It's more of a *zing* than a whistle. The movies got it all wrong. It sounds like the sky is unzipping itself.

When an American F-16 mistakenly drops a two-thousand-pound bomb on your platoon—a bomb with a two percent failure rate—you don't forget it. But it becomes more of a big deal later. When it happens, you just think, *wow, that was close,* and you leave it at that. You think, *somebody better tell those motherfuckers to redirect.*

It's not until later that it starts to work on your head. A two-thousand-pound bomb falls on you and the chance that you get to continue living at that moment is one in fifty. It's only when you get home that the idea that you should be dead begins to creep in.

The fog of war in Baghdad rapidly deteriorated into the fog of looting and anarchy. People were using whatever they could to move furniture and the like—cars filled to their ceilings, little white pickup trucks with beds stacked four feet high. I saw two guys driving a yellow front-end loader—the front end of which was loaded with filing cabinets and tables. When this happened, Secretary Rumsfeld, a man with no combat experience, just raised his eyebrows, squinted, and remarked smugly, "Freedom is untidy."

We were clearing two walled Baath Party estates that had been squeezed between the Tigris and the refinery. Someone had bombed the hell out of the first building I entered. One had missed—landing in the back yard by pool, leaving a crater fifteen feet in diameter. Another had not. It had been a direct hit, blowing off most of the backside of the mansion. The blast had shredded the sides, leaving only the very front somewhat as it had looked before the explosion. Concrete and sandstone hung precipitously from what was left of the second story, while spindly strands of reinforcing steel round bar delicately held large chunks of the ruined structure together. The front columns were cracked and had shifted in places, giving them an ancient Greek look. They seemed desperate to maintain control of the building's crumbling façade.

We only hesitated for a moment—out of concern for a possible collapse—before going in. When we did, we found there was nothing left. We went through every single room in the place, walking over and sifting through rubble in each one. From the debris, I was able to pull a single brass door handle. Everything else had been looted. Furniture, light fixtures, electrical outlets, wiring, doorknobs, everything.

As we were picking through the ruins, Sergeant Croom came in from the other compound. The first thing he said to me was, "Don't go in the back yard. Motherfuckers'll shoot at you from across the river."

After a while I walked out of the crumbling front door onto the soft, green grass that made up the front yard. I wanted to see the other mansion. There were bits and pieces of the house covering the lawn, having been ejected during the blast. I walked out, walked down some cracked steps, onto the grass, and then stepped off a four-foot drop-off. I was right beside my truck. Someone had adorned the hood of it with an Iraqi helmet.

I thought about Croom's advice. *Motherfuckers'll shoot at you from across the river.* As I walked past the mansion in which I'd just been, I could barely see to the other side of the river—

the property was raised about four feet, shielding me from the back of the house and beyond. As I moved closer to the gate, the raised portion sloped to an end. In front of me was a sixty-foot span through which I would have to move in plain view of the river. It looked to have been about four hundred yards from where I stood to the other side of the river.

I stood there for a minute weighing the chances. I didn't think anyone could hit a moving target with an AK-47 at over four hundred yards. But I was still hesitant. I was wondering if perhaps today just wasn't my day.

Then I thought about all the soldiers who had gone before me in wars past—soldiers who had moved through withering barrages of machine gun fire at close range, dodging hand grenades at every step. I thought about it and wanted to slap myself for being such a pussy.

I stepped out from behind the cover, wanting to move quickly, but still casually enough to look cool in case anybody I knew was watching. I moved in a sort of ambling shuffle. Then, halfway across the sixty-foot expanse, I heard the crack of the rifle. My head ducked instinctively and I kept moving, safely making it to the other side. I hadn't felt the bullet or heard an impact—which was about what I would expect from someone with an AK from that far away. Nowhere close. But it was there. Somebody had been watching—and waiting.

The new building was far less exciting than the first one. It hadn't been bombed, and that has a lot to do with how fun it is to explore a place. When I walked back to the gap between the properties that offered no cover, I didn't hesitate. I didn't sprint, but I didn't shuffle either. It was more of a *stride*. With my M4 in my right hand, my left arm outstretched toward the river, and my middle finger raised defiantly, I ran. This time there was only the sound of boots clocking on concrete and labored breathing.

It almost hurt my feelings.

Later that afternoon we found ourselves back in the field with the anti-aircraft guns. Delta Company had been tasked with cleaning up the debris, mostly the unused ammunition. We were stacking the 57mm rounds in the beds of the humvees when Captain B. received a call on the radio that the scout sniper team on the second floor of the mansion was currently exchanging fire with somebody on the ground floor of the building. The Voice simply told him to bail them out—and fast.

Captain B. stepped out of his truck, still gripping the outstretched hand mike. There were several of us who had been standing near him during the conversation. He was obviously flustered, his face becoming redder by the second as it always did when he was pissed. He look at the group of us and asked, "Does anybody know how the hell to get there from here?"

"Yeah, I know how to get there," I replied, putting on my helmet. "We spent over an hour there this afternoon."

"Okay. We're leaving in thirty seconds."

Soft dirt and green grass were churned up as Sergeant Whipple, in the lead, sped out of the field as if his truck had been fired from a cannon. We drove in a line toward the refinery, Captain B. and Corporal Davis in tow.

During the frantic drive a radio call informed me that the shooting had ceased. It said that the scouts had exchanged gunfire, driving off the looters. They said they had fired shots, hitting the looters' vehicle as it sped away. But for some reason, still holed up on the second floor, now the scouts suspected the looters had returned.

When we pulled to a stop in front of the mansion, everyone poured out of their vehicles and ran like in the TV show *Cops*. Somewhere along the way, formal infantry tactics had fallen by the wayside.

By the time I made it to the foyer, Sergeant Estrada was already hauling a looter out of the mansion with a firm grip on the man's arm. Behind him, my guys hustled two other looters outside. One was a woman.

Within seconds they were seated side by side, flex-cuffed and with bags on their heads. I went in to try to figure out just what in the hell was going on. The first thing I noticed was that the car outside didn't match the description I'd gotten over the radio. The second was that these three didn't have a single weapon. And third, one was a girl wearing jeans and a t-shirt.

Captain B. had spoken with the scouts. It seemed that the sandbagged detainees sitting helplessly on the sidewalk had walked into the wrong place at a very bad time.

Nobody knew what to do with them, whether or not they had weapons. At that point we knew how to do only two things: kill or ignore. But if that had been combat math, then this was turning into combat calculus. Now, on a breezy April afternoon in Baghdad, we had just entered the biggest gray area since Vietnam.

Croom was standing near the unlucky looters. "What do we do now? I mean . . . what the fuck?" I asked when I got to him. We couldn't just call the police and have them come pick them up. There were no police. And these people weren't your standard enemy combatants either.

He just shrugged and said, "Fuck if I know."

I looked down at the three, all of whom had their had hands tied behind their backs. I saw that the girl was shaking. The two guys sitting next to her were squirming nervously. For the first time I noticed they were all wearing jeans, t-shirts, and tennis shoes. And sandbags. They looked harmless.

Suddenly one of the men spoke up. In heavily accented but understandable English, he asked his question in a quivering voice—one that hinted of guilt-ridden blame—as if it had been his idea to come here and he felt responsible for his two friends.

Through the dark-colored sandbag he turned his head up to us and asked, "Are you going to execute us?" He asked it in a tone that conveyed his expecting the worst. The man was convinced he was about to die.

Are you going to execute us?

I stopped breathing for an instant, trying to figure out if he was joking or not. I realized that he was not. I glanced at Sergeant Croom, trying to think of a way to respond. Puzzled, Croom looked back at me with raised eyebrows.

He looked down at the guy without missing a beat. "*Execute* you? Naw way, man," he said in his Southern drawl. "We're Americans." He looked up shifting his eyes to the river. "We don't do that shit."

The looter pointed his head back at the ground and simply nodded, as if he weren't sure if we were going to tell him the truth or not.

It's funny—Croom's answer, while said offhandedly, had actually meant something to me. His tone had punched a hole in my cynical shell. It meant that the way things were done in this city had changed. The executions had ceased as of the last forty-eight hours. There would be no more throwing people off buildings, no more cutting off ears or cutting out tongues. There would be no more mass graves. It was just over.

The optimism we felt that day would wilt in the coming months, as most of Iraq would become a menagerie of freakish horror. But for just that day, for just that *week*, the people there were free.

An hour later we let them go, telling them not to go into any more abandoned buildings. When Sergeant Krueger handed them the keys to their car the girl broke down sobbing. One of the men held her. The other man, who had at one point told us he had lived in Buffalo, broke into a wide grin. He looked like he was going to start jumping up and down. All three of them were still shaking like leaves. As they helped the girl into the front seat, the English speaker started rambling to Croom and me excitedly. He thanked us over and over, letting us know how appreciative of us he was, and how he would never loot anything ever again.

In two wars I'd seen plenty of people who thought they were going to die. But it was always something abstract. These people, however, had been convinced that they were going to be shot with their hands tied behind their backs in the next few minutes. Witnessing their emotional roller coaster for an hour actually made my stomach turn. This was too much—too much power and too much reality. I'd been in two wars, literally joking my way through combat both times, without ever firing a shot. Even when I had known that my chances of dying were raised, there had still been room for humor of that special, macabre sort. But now it wasn't so funny anymore. Everything over the past year and a half had been at such a *distance*. Now it was so close. Now I could see the expressions of fear and hear the cracking voices of those subject to my authority—those civilians caught in the midst of combat. *They had been so scared.*

This wasn't what I'd been trained for. I didn't want this. It confused me. *Where was the* real *enemy?*

For the first time I wanted to lay down my weapon and go home for a reason other than fear. What was I doing ten thousand miles from home, scaring a woman and two men out of their minds—to the point that they thought they were going to die? It was *their* country and *I* was the stranger. They had had absolutely nothing to do with yellow cake from Africa, chemical weapons, or 9/11, and yet, here we were pushing them around, exerting our power over them. This wasn't what I was there for.

On the way back to the refinery I couldn't get the image of that beleaguered horse in the Shah-e-Kot Valley out of my head. Like the looters, it too had been unwittingly caught up in events.

For several days I watch the animal as mortars and bombs continue to fall. It is an innocent horse trapped in the crossfire of humans working around the clock to slaughter each other. At times the horse seems placid, content to wait us out. Sometimes I think it is actually unaware of what is happening around it. But then, inevitably, a mortar round lands too close—either by accident or because a sadistic spotter calls it in—and the horse gives itself away by running and bucking and shaking its head wildly. Watching through binoculars it looks as if the animal is being driven insane by the sounds and concussions.

And then, after a while, it settles down, probably thinking to itself that this can't last forever.

Seeing a living thing standing alone in the Valley was strange. It was so out of place there as explosives rained down and snipers' bullets zipped back and forth. It didn't seem fair. At night, I would listen to the Spectre gunship descend on the area and unleash its wrath. In the morning, I would always expect to see the carcass of what had been a lonely, frightened, and abandoned horse. Instead, I would see it standing on the valley floor, nose to the ground, looking for something to eat on the thawing soil. Just trying to live.

As the sun started sinking, we started winding down. I had my platoon consolidate with the rest of the battalion on the grounds of the refinery. There was an air of euphoria around the place. The thirteen-year-old conflict between the United States and Iraq seemed to be over.

Someone from Alpha Company had cracked open a fire hydrant. I hadn't seen running water in nearly a month and it reminded me that I hadn't really bathed in that time either.

After my first shower in the fire hydrant, I went and sat down on a curb, soaking up the day's last rays and drying out. I heard yelling and looked up, reflexively reaching for my M4. I saw three freshly showered guys from Alpha Company wearing not a stitch of clothing between them, chasing and tormenting each other with their wet, twisted brown t-shirts. They were trying to smack each other on the ass. I thought maybe this meant we were near the end.

* * *

Dusk was setting in an hour later and I was standing outside my humvee eating a granola bar when the evening call to prayer commenced over a loudspeaker. The sounds of the muezzin were lilting, unlike the scratchy chanting I'd had to endure in Pakistan. The singing mixed with the sound of rustling leaves in a tree that towered over the refinery grounds. Had circumstances been different, the evening breeze and the sound of the prayers could have put me to sleep. Instead, I just stood there taking it in. Beyond the walls of the refinery I could see the beige dome of a small mosque from which I assumed the call was emanating. It sounded so peaceful—the sounds of gunfire having been replaced by calls to pray.

Then I noticed the smoke on the horizon behind the mosque. Two distinct plumes—probably oil fires, were still burning in the distance. The contrast was strikingly ominous. As I listened to the music and watched the black smoke waft over the city, I had a feeling in the pit of my stomach—as if we'd broken something and didn't yet realize it. The call to prayer seemed a sign of normalcy—and of tranquility. But standing there snacking on my granola bar and looking at the evening sky, I began to feel uneasy—as if the smoke were somehow casting a pall on our success. On the surface, everything seemed great. The crackle of gunfire had diminished, along with the periodic explosions. But there was something in the way the oily smoke drifted silently beyond the mosque. It was almost an instinct, I guess—an instinct that told me we had been very naïve in coming to this place.

The war melted away. There was no announcement, no Army-wide proclamation; there was just being shot at one day, and the next day things were just *different*. Traffic began picking up. Shops started reopening and people began venturing out from their homes without the intention of pillaging.

I spent most of my second day in Baghdad tracking down the unexploded ordnance deposited by air force and navy aircraft—along with that left by the retreating Iraqi Army.

That day was like a big Easter egg hunt. We didn't know it at the time, but we were actually competing with future insurgents to see who could collect the most Easter eggs by dark. Throughout the afternoon we found unexploded bombs, artillery pieces, caches of RPGs, and piles of anti-aircraft ammunition. Most of it we couldn't transport in our humvees, so we just copied down the GPS coordinate for the piece in question and marked it on a map. Then we left, never to see it again.

Late that afternoon, I was told by Captain B. of a reported "debris field" adjacent to the Daura Expressway. He told me to go and occupy the field with my platoon until the explosive ordnance disposal guys showed up. Basically, just to go there, hang out, and keep the natives away from anything that looked dangerous.

To deal with the Iraqis, I brought along a female linguist who had been sent to us by Brigade. I was looking forward to having someone relieve the stress that comes with communicating through hand signals and facial expressions.

We arrived at the so-called debris field just as the sun was beginning to set. It was an open area of short grass and hard-packed dirt. The field was a square about three hundred yards on each side. Apartments bordered it on two sides. Initially I noticed two soccer goals on the field, along with groups of Iraqis going to and from the apartments.

Then, as my eyes adjusted to seeking out weaponry, I began to see it.

The field was covered with ammunition in varying conditions. I could see two shattered artillery pieces nearby. It only took me a second to figure out that the Iraqi Army had emplaced a battery of anti-aircraft artillery pieces on the neighborhood soccer field. I could see that it had all been pulverized. The ground was a patchwork of littered ammunition that had been blown sky high during the attack.

We were walking through a garden in which highly explosive weeds grew. As I moved through the field, I noticed a piece of unexploded ordnance off to my left. It was big, yellow, and dented. It wasn't shaped like a regular bomb in that it was more squarish rather than long. Stepping carefully, I thought of the words "Fat Man" and "Little Boy." It had been dropped with the intent of destroying an expansive area. Now it just sat there.

Within a minute of our stopping vehicles, two hundred people were swarming the platoon. Every kid in the neighborhood wanted to see the Americans up close. I hurried to find the linguist, hoping that she could say something that would stem the rising tide of potential shrapnel recipients. I could just see a kid stepping on a leftover cluster bomblet next to me, sending us all to hell.

An older kid in a striped shirt came up to me and asked in broken English if I spoke French. When I said I didn't, he managed to make clear that he had someone he wanted me to meet. He left for a second and then brought back another guy, this one with his left arm in a sling.

The French speaker then managed to get across that the injured boy had been caught in the American bombing of this area several days earlier. He said he'd been hit with shrapnel. As he said it, he reached toward the other boy and pulled down his shirt, revealing a row of stitches and dried blood on his chest.

He paused, looking at me. Then he pointed to an apartment building and said, "Two children . . . from there . . . killed in same attack." He looked me in the eye. "You should not kill children."

I didn't know what to say. Sorry? Does that cut it? I was skeptical but I decided to give it a try. "Sorry."

The kid must have sensed the awkwardness for me because he suddenly declared, "George Boosh, good." Then he continued "But you will understand," he said, his eyes again meeting mine, "this is very hard for us."

I had to say something then, so I just said, "I know."

At the time that was more or less a lie, since I didn't know. I couldn't have known. Americans cannot comprehend what the Iraqi people have been through for the last five, fifteen, or thirty-five years.

Take an average Iraqi family in Baghdad for instance. You live for twenty years under the reign of Saddam Hussein. During that time daily life is okay. You get an excellent education at Baghdad University, the electricity is always on, and there's plenty of food. But you're cut off from the world—and your city is ruled by the secret police. You can't say anything against the government lest you risk having your family tortured and killed. Even if you do support the government, there's nothing to say you couldn't run into Uday or Qusay Hussein one night at a restaurant—and that Uday couldn't take a liking to your fifteen-year-old daughter. You lead an oppressive existence, but for the most part, it's bearable.

Then Saddam invades Kuwait. You talk about it over dinner with your family, and here, in the privacy of your own home, you all decide that this could be disastrous for Iraq. After the war, the United Nations, led by the United States, imposes harsh sanctions on Iraq. At first you think maybe there is a silver lining—that maybe this will force Saddam to change his ways. But then the food becomes rationed—along with the electricity and the gasoline. The supply of medicine in the hospital dries up too. You go to the dentist for a toothache and he tells you it needs to be pulled. You say okay. But then he tells you there's no anesthetic. It's the sanctions, he says.

For twelve long years you live like this—in a city under siege. The thought of a foreign invader coming to handle your own problems is painful to you because you are a proud Iraqi. But with two healthy children and one sick child, your family cannot bear to live like this much longer. Whether you are Sunni, Shia, or Kurd, you begin to wish that the Americans would come. At the very least, their coming could not make life worse than it already is under the sanctions.

Finally, the first bombs begin to fall. Terrified, you huddle with your family and your dog on the first floor of your home. You've barricaded yourselves with cushions from the couches because that's all you have. As the bombs rattle the windows, through your fear, you think that Saddam and his thug government are finally getting what they deserve.

Within days Saddam's government flees. You are hopeful, but you still sleep with your family on the first floor. One night you know the Americans are near—you can hear the shooting. You hear a tank rumbling through your neighborhood. You hear it fire once, and the sound is incredible—it's deafening. It fires again. But this time the round strikes close, shattering every window in your house. The next morning, while sweeping up the glass outside, you find that the

American tank round landed in your neighbor's house, killing his wife and two daughters.

Distraught, you confront the first American you see on foot the next day. You want to ask him what happened—you want to know how this could occur. Don't the Americans have satellites and lasers to guide their weapons? As you approach the young man in desert camouflage, the first thing he does is point his rifle straight at your chest. You can see that he is more terrified and confused than you are. You show him that you're not a threat and continue moving in his direction. He screams something at you in English and fires a shot in the air. You plead with him in Arabic that you only want to talk to someone. That is when he comes over and throws you on the ground pointing his weapon at your head. Your family comes outside, crying.

Lying there, your face in the dust and your lip now bleeding, you wonder how things have ended up this way.

Eventually the wounded kid blended back in with the crowd. In the end, we abandoned the debris field before any ordnance disposal people arrived to take over. It was getting dark and I wasn't going to allow my platoon to become stranded in a minefield after nightfall. We left all of the ammunition and artillery pieces where they lay.

Dealing with this unexploded weaponry became a way of life in Baghdad. But in a city blanketed with all types of hardware originally primed to explode on contact, you knew it was going to happen.

I remember blowing through traffic trying to get to the site of the blast. The road down which we drove, like all the others in Baghdad, was dusty and crawling with little kids playing in the late afternoon sun. On our right was a row of homes—the southern edge of a neighborhood. To our left was an open field, strewn with bricks and garbage. All I could see ahead of us were the tall palm trees that meant we were close to the Tigris—and the farms along the river. We drove into the forest.

Arriving at the scene, I jumped out of my truck in a street that had suddenly become nothing more than a narrow alleyway. Immediately I could see that my platoon's presence there would have a minor effect at best. Events were already in motion and there was nothing I could do to alter them. As I stepped out, the first thing I noticed among the moving soldiers and growing crowd of onlookers were the footprints on the dusty ground.

They were bloody footprints. But it wasn't like somebody got some blood on his foot and then walked around leaving partial prints. These were solid crimson footprints. I could see every single toe. I could see the entire outline of the foot—where it narrowed at the arch, and then where it widened and curved back into the heel. They had come from an open gate to our right. I followed them in reverse for ten or fifteen feet. Walking inside the gate, I noticed the prints went as far back along the concrete path as I could see. They were spaced widely apart—as if the man had been running and bleeding profusely at the same time. I turned and followed them back out on the street. This time, though, I followed them to their source.

He was an Iraqi civilian and he was lying on his back, nearly naked. He wasn't moving, and there was blood everywhere. Kneeling over him and working feverishly were two sergeants I recognized from Charlie Company. Sergeant Salido was bent over the man trying to insert an IV into his right arm, in a last desperate attempt to replenish his limp body with fluid. At the same time, Sergeant Iosefo was performing CPR.

Watching his hands and his face as he worked, I could see desperation beginning to work its way into Salido's movements. The man's circulatory system was rapidly failing and Salido couldn't find a vein. Suddenly he looked up and cried out, "I can't find a vein! I can't . . . ." His eyes were searching for anyone who could help him. For some reason I noticed he was still wearing his glasses. Then, for a brief second, we made eye contact, and I stood there, frozen.

Salido knew that no one could help him. We were all the same there—everyone was nearly equally ignorant in how to treat traumatic injuries. His statement seemed to have been posed more out of exasperation than anything else—as if he were trying to preemptively explain to the universe why the man was going to die. As he went back to work, I noticed that the man's eyes had already rolled back in his head.

Sergeant Iosefo was across from Salido, trying to perform mouth-to-mouth. He pumped one, two, three, and then bent over to breathe into the dying man's mouth. I watched him do this three times. But then the man's lungs began to fill with fluid, and the next time Iosefo blew into his lungs, the man began to vomit. Iosefo kept going. He kept pounding on the man's chest and breathing, pounding and breathing, until finally, he started to gag himself on the man's vomit. Gasping and coughing, he finally quit and sat back. Iosefo didn't move—he just sat there next to the body, staring straight ahead. By that time, Salido had also stopped. He dropped the man's arm and stood up.

A black cloud of flies then descended on the body. It was as though they had been courteous enough to allow the Americans some time to save the man before diving in to feast on the fresh blood. It was as if they had done this before—like they were laughing at our naiveté, at our surprise that people really did die. *Save that guy?,* they buzzed. *Are you kidding? Couldn't you tell ten minutes ago that he was going to die by the way his body temperature dropped as soon as he hit the ground? By the way his eyes rolled back in his head? This is Baghdad, sheltered Americans. Get used to it.* One of my soldiers quickly grabbed his camouflaged poncho and covered the Iraqi.

I never saw the wounded Americans. They had remained inside the gate. All I knew was that one of them had been a new guy, a new platoon leader actually, named Bilotta. I had only met him two days earlier while he was on his first patrol with his platoon. He was a big guy and a former West Pointer who, when I met him, seemed to be in the fog of confusion that envelops new officers when they first take command. He was instantly likeable, though, and had seemed eager to get started. From what I could gather, his legs were now somewhat shredded by fragmentation.

Once the scene had been cleared, and onlookers and hysterical family members had been placated, we headed back to the palace to which we'd moved that morning. When we arrived, everything was normal. Guys were lounging and listening to music and some were sitting on cots eating MREs. The rest were sweeping and clearing away debris in order to make their new home livable.

While I was sitting alone on my cot, staring at CDs I had no real interest in listening to, Phil came over. He was taking a break from fixing up his area and came to ask if I could get a picture of him standing next to the indoor pool they had discovered while exploring the grounds. I said sure and we walked across the courtyard to the pool house. As we approached the steps leading up to it, Phil turned to me and asked, "So what'd you guys do today? Anything interesting?" He hadn't heard about the UXO incident.

"Well," I said, "I just watched a guy die right in front of me. That was interesting."

He said, "Who, wha—American or Iraqi?"

"Iraqi," I answered. "Civilian."

His face turned serious. "You . . . I mean, you okay?"

Suddenly, out of nowhere, for just a split second, I wasn't okay. I thought I was going to get choked up. But then the feeling passed as quickly as it had come. "Yeah, fine," I said. "Where do you want me to take your picture?"

The first time I watched something die I was fourteen years old. I had a pellet gun that I used for paper targets and for shooting pine cones out of trees. One day I had a friend over who also liked to shoot. Except when it was his turn, he chose to aim at a blue jay that had landed on the fence. The bird never saw it coming. My friend hit it with a single shot, dropping the bird onto the grass below. I was horrified, but didn't say anything.

We walked over to the wounded animal and knelt down beside it. The hole was large, I thought, for a pellet. Its heart was still pumping and I could see the afternoon sun glinting off the bright red blood that was pooling in the bird's chest. The blue jay was gasping and convulsing, its eyes shifting in pain and fear. I wanted to do something to help, but knew that

I couldn't. We watched as the bird slowly became still. My friend just picked it up by the legs and threw it over the fence without another thought.

That day in Baghdad was kind of the same thing.

The translator's name was Ammar. Ammar was twenty-six years old and single, and he liked women, American movies, and beer—in no particular order. As Baghdad became a blur of raids, guard duty, and civil assistance, I'd gotten to know this son of a retired Iraqi general. He was a portly, good-natured computer science guy with a thick black moustache.

Ammar had come to the unit just after our arrival in Baghdad. His family was middle class, and like all the other translators, he began his work with us very informally. There was no real process for hiring translators at that time. Most either approached American units on patrol or simply appeared at the gates looking for work. If their spoken English was good enough, they were then run through a battery of verbal questions in order to properly vet them. The questions asked of each applicant usually went something like this:

1. Do you like Americans?

2. Will you work for five U.S. dollars a day?

3. Are you a religious fundamentalist, Chechen rebel, ETA bomber, Tamil Tiger, IRA assassin, al Qaeda operative, Hezbollah rocketeer, Hamas bus bomber, Zapatista, Crip, Blood, Ku Klux Klansman, abortion clinic bomber, member of either Jemaah Islamiyah, Abu Sayyaf, Ansar al Islam, Aryan Nation, the Jewish Defense League, the Symbionese Liberation Army, or any other type of terrorist not previously mentioned?

4. Will you show up for work on time?

Questions regarding the Baath Party were conspicuously absent. Typical responses were yes, yes, no, and yes.

Ammar was always hanging around our compound, talking to anyone who'd listen. Sometimes he'd even use one of our dry-erase boards to teach Arabic to the guys. He couldn't get enough of the fact that he was actually getting to work with *real* American soldiers. Like me, he'd seen too many movies. Except the difference was that in his case, they'd taught him English.

The first raid my platoon did with Ammar was a hunt for one of Saddam's "nephews." Since we'd gotten to Baghdad, it seemed to me that most raids conducted by the battalion were precipitated by a tip of doubtful provenance that was going to lead us to one of Saddam's nefarious and on-the-run nephews. Yet no matter how much high-tech equipment we used, no one could ever bag a nephew.

That week we were attached to the battalion headquarters as part of a quick-reaction force. According the captain for whom I was working, the nephew was supposed to be at a pool hall on a street lined with shops and apartments. With no margin for error in such a tight environment, Croom, Ammar, and I spent the morning rehearsing with the platoon how it would go down later that afternoon. First we had to make sure that we were going to hit the right building, and second, we had to ensure that our timing was down for all the moving pieces. It was the first mission I'd ever done where I had the privilege of getting overhead satellite imagery of the location beforehand—even though the copied photos of Daura's center looked like nothing but urban mush.

We left in a two-platoon convoy from the Daura refinery when the sun was at its peak that day. My platoon was to raid the pool hall, while Phil's platoon would seal off the neighborhood block. As we closed on the suspected location, my truck and Estrada's truck peeled off from the formation. While the rest of the convoy continued to drive around the neighborhood, Estrada and I went to "casually" case the pool hall with a quick drive-by. There were people everywhere on the bustling street—kids were crowding kebab stands, men were making deals at butcher shops for fresh meat hanging in the windows, and women on apartment balconies were hanging clothes out to dry. And just where I'd expected it to be was an open door through which I was able to barely, but unmistakably, distinguish a pool cue being passed around as we cruised past. While turning the corner at the next intersection, I radioed the positive ID to the rest of the team. This was a relief—usually it was more of guess as to whether we were headed into the right building or not.

We linked up with the rest of the group a few blocks away and wasted no time in moving back to the pool hall. This time we weren't so casual about it. Croom and Whipple's section sped down the busy thoroughfare and quickly blocked traffic on either side of the pool hall by parking sideways in the middle of the street. They dismounted immediately and took up positions behind their trucks. Iraqis started hustling to get out of the way, taking this as the cue for an impending shootout. My truck followed Estrada's section and we screeched to a halt right outside the front door. Textbook.

Estrada leapt out of his truck and headed for the door. Following right behind his guys, I could see out of the side of my eye as Ammar came running toward us. He was wearing blue jeans and a striped, short-sleeve, collared shirt. Coming from Croom's vehicle, he was covering the distance as fast as his hefty legs would carry him. As I moved, I noticed that not all the civilians had cleared the street, and that some were still standing and watching the event take place.

The light was dim inside the pool hall. For some odd reason, the patrons didn't react. They just stopped playing, straightened up, and looked at us. They weren't sure yet whether or not they were in trouble. Neither was I. Estrada went with Ammar to the rear of the building first, while I stayed near the entrance. Through the awkward silence that followed, I could hear Ammar asking in Arabic about the nephew. An Iraqi standing close by just stared at me. I was covered in sweat from head to toe standing there holding a gun. From behind my Wiley-X sunglasses, I looked down and saw that he had been about to break the rack. Now he just stood there, pool cue in hand and unsure of what to do now. I had the urge to ask him, "So . . . do you like, come here often?"

In less than a minute we were back out front, Ammar and Estrada having escorted the owner from his office in the back. I could tell by the look on Ammar's face that something was wrong. As we walked the guy over to the captain for questioning, I asked Ammar, "What's up man? Dry hole?"

He said, "I don't know yet. Something funny."

Always something funny. I stood at the entrance of an alley watching the conversation. By the shrugs and flailing arms of the pool hall owner, and the slumping shoulders, eye rolls, and neck cranes of the captain, I could clearly see that this raid, like most others we'd done, was about nothing.

While we were waiting for things to get sorted out, I stood next to Phil on the sidewalk, beneath the overhang of a shop. Guys from both of our platoons were milling about, keeping the growing crowd of Iraqi kids at bay. I noticed that right next to us, the kids kept getting closer and closer—and that it was starting to agitate one of Phil's younger sergeants. They were pushing in and giggling, asking the standard, "What ees your name, meester?"

I was only halfheartedly keeping an eye on the kids when I heard Phil's sergeant suddenly get gruff with them. "Get the fuck back!" he bellowed. "I said get the fuck back!" I turned to look at him. I was trying to figure out why he was getting upset, when he suddenly reached out and shoved the Iraqi closest to him, knocking the boy to the ground. The boy landed on his ass with an "Ummph." The rest of the kids stopped talking, looked at the sergeant, and then moved quickly to help up their friend. They'd stopped giggling.

For the first time in two wars, I completely lost my mind. I stepped between the sergeant and the boy, getting right in the sergeant's face. I noticed he was an inch or two taller than me. "What the fuck are you . . . goddamn! . . . fucking stupid! . . . Jesus Christ! . . . create fucking terrorists! . . . turn this whole goddamn city against us with that kind of shit! . . . fucking bully! . . . gonna create more problems than you could ever deal with! . . . making terrorists! . . . don't ever let me see that kind of shit . . . god*damn*!

Everyone within a twenty-five-foot radius had gone silent in the afternoon sun. I couldn't tell who looked more surprised—the sergeant, the Iraqi kids, or Phil. They all just stood there, staring at me, waiting to see what I would do next.

I shook my head, turned my back, and walked off a few feet. Our collective frustration was starting to build.

When Ammar finally came back to me he explained that the tipster was a business rival who thought he could get the other guy's pool hall shut down by associating it with Saddam.

I thought about that and realized that the guy's plan had actually almost worked. That was how raids went in Baghdad—one guy would feed bad information to the Americans so that we would mess with a guy that had messed with him.

The next night Croom suggested we go have dinner with Ammar's family at their house in Daura. He was a sucker for home cooking. At first I was hesitant, but then considered that we deserved it after another wasted raid that afternoon. An old guy had come to us at a traffic control point and given Ammar and Croom a tip. This time it was a weapons cache belonging to one of Saddam's men, who also happened to be the guy's neighbor.

When we pulled "Saddam's man" and his terrified family from their home and out into their front yard, the women and children were sobbing uncontrollably in standard raid fashion. The guy didn't know what the fuck was going on. Then something dawned on him and he asked Ammar if this had anything to do with his neighbor.

My shoulders had slumped, defeated.

This time it was about a feud over a staircase. "Saddam's man" had built a staircase that went up to his roof along the side of his house. The problem was, that on the staircase, you could see down onto the next-door property. He told us that, aside from being paranoid and senile, the old guy had become quite upset recently and accused him of spying on the man's wife and daughters. I looked over at the guy's huddled, crying family. I was sure that they expected we were about to cart their husband and father off to Abu Ghraib over a dispute with their neighbor.

I took one look at Croom and could see sweat running in rivulets down his bald head—probably from the combination of embarrassment and frustration. I tapped him on the arm. "Come on, man. Let's get the fuck outta here. We're wasting our time."

Four words: *Weapons of Mass Destruction*. Five more words: *What a bunch of shit.*

Between the fall of Saddam and everything eventually devolving into chaos, you could eat dinner inside Iraqi houses without having to worry about the family being attacked for aiding the enemy. All you had to do was put one or two guys out front with the humvees for security.

Ammar's house was an oasis of sort-of-normal life in the midst of a sort-of-war. He lived in a two-story house with his mother, father, brother, sister, and their giant brown dog, not far from the highway. With his father, he'd watched from the front yard while the 3rd Infantry Division had fought its way into the city.

Watching his mother prepare the food in the kitchen while at the same time ordering everyone around, I realized that I'd never been inside an Iraqi's house when I wasn't turning over cushions or opening closets looking for guns and RPGs. It was sitting there at the kitchen table, trying to act like a human for the first time in a while, that I noticed something that made the war seem ridiculous.

On the refrigerator, Ammar's family had magnets. Some of them held photos in place. Two of them affixed a drawing done by a child. It looked like the refrigerator I'd grown up with at my parents' house. I wondered what we were doing fighting people with magnets on their refrigerators.

When we weren't going on wild goose chases or eating chicken and couscous at Ammar's house, we were either guarding something or providing some form of civil assistance. During that time Croom and Ammar had become friends, and Ammar was working almost exclusively with our platoon. But the workload became too much and we needed some more Iraqi help.

I met the new guy late one afternoon at the Daura police station. Mohamed was a freshly minted civil engineer from the University of Baghdad. He looked nearly Western in his blue jeans, white t-shirt, goatee, sideburns, and wire-rimmed glasses. He'd heard that the Americans were hiring translators.

Within a couple of hours of meeting him, we managed to cover politics, religion, war, foreign relations, and cooking. Like so many young Iraqis, he was overly eager to tell his story to someone from the West—to inform the free world that he and the rest of his peers were, for the most part, not chemical weapon-toting holy warriors.

We talked about the merits of the invasion. Mohamed said that it had been a good idea. Whenever he spoke of Saddam or his henchmen, his face crinkled like he wanted to puke. But Mohamed was also concerned with the Israeli-Palestinian issue. He wanted to know why the Americans always seemed to side with the Israelis.

About that time a guy came into the police station looking for us. Somebody in the neighborhood behind the station had found a UXO and they wanted help. I tried to think of a way out of dealing with it—but I couldn't come up with anything.

"Hey Mohamed," I said. "You want to go check this out with me? It could be interesting."

"Yes, man, of course!" He seemed flattered that I'd asked for his help. I went outside and got Sergeant Croom. In turn, he wrangled two of our guys to bring along. The informant had said something to Mohamed and pointed us in the general direction of some houses. Together, the five of us walked outside to the back of the police station and set out across a small open field.

We stuck to a heavily trodden dirt trail, so as to avoid mistakenly finding any UXOs of our own. Not halfway across the field I saw a man standing near a house, under the shade of a stand of trees. He was waving us over.

We approached cautiously. On the ground at his feet, the Iraqi pointed to something small and yellow. It looked like it was made out of plastic.

"Mohamed, tell him to get away from it. And ask him where it came from." I had a bad habit of talking to my translator instead of talking directly to the person.

There was an exchange in Arabic. Then Mohamed turned to me. "He says an airplane dropped it. He doesn't know what it is."

I noticed the guy inching closer to it. It was making me uncomfortable. The thing looked to me the like it might have been part of a plastic toy or something, but I wasn't taking any chances. "Mohamed, I said tell him get back from it." I was getting agitated and the guy was now bending over it.

Croom took a step back. "Hey man," he said. "Tell that motherfucker to back up!"

Mohamed said something in Arabic to the guy. Then the guy smiled at us revealing a mangled set of teeth. But he didn't move.

"Hey Mohamed, what's he doing?"

Mohamed said something in Arabic again.

Suddenly the guy reached down and picked the object up.

"Hey, what the fuck! Drop that motherfucker!" I screamed, raising my weapon. I started moving backward. Mohamed started shouting at the guy and the guy started talking back to him, all the while smiling and shaking the yellow object. I noticed Croom scooting near a tree, trying to get behind it. In my mind I quickly started trying to work out the combat calculus that would tell me how to deal with this.

Then Croom called out: "Hey . . . hey, Mohamed . . . tell . . . tell that motherfucker that shit's not funny, man!" His voice was that of grown man about piss his pants.

"Mohamed," I yelled, "I'm gonna shoot this motherfucker if he doesn't drop that thing *right now*! Mohamed, do something!" I was nearly beside myself. Rather than continuing to slowly back up, I started backpedaling at a quicker pace, still pointing my weapon at the guy. The two privates with us were already way behind me. Croom stayed behind the tree, now too afraid to move out into the open.

Everybody was yelling at the same time. I didn't want to have to shoot this guy over a misunderstanding, but dying for this guy's stupidity was not an option either. This was the same thing that had happened to Charlie Company and the Iraqi who had died right in front of me. Given the choice, I would shoot first and ask questions later. This was not how I was going to die.

Mohamed hadn't backed up all that far. He continued to bicker with the man. Suddenly I saw Mohamed raise his arms. He was standing in the middle of a potential crossfire. In front of him was a smiling man with a possible explosive. Behind him were four Americans ready to waste that man. Arms held high, he said, "Wait, wait, Friedman . . . I think this guy is fucking with you. Nobody shoot."

From a hundred feet away I called out in response. "Why? What'd he tell you?" I could see Croom hunkered down, still behind the tree.

"I think he is fucking with us, man. I don't think it's anything. There's something wrong with this guy," Mohamed explained, his arms still raised.

"No shit there's something wrong with this guy," Croom chimed in from his position behind the tree.

"Friedman, really, I think we should leave. This guy is crazy or something," Mohamed yelled to me over the distance.

Seemingly out of the blast range, I yelled back, "Fine. Great." I looked at Croom and gave him the head nod. He took one more look at the guy before stepping gingerly from behind the tree and moving quickly toward the open field with his weapon raised.

As we trotted back to the police station, I looked back and saw the guy with the plastic toy or whatever it was still smiling at us.

It left me with an eerie feeling.

Before I left the station that day, I asked Mohamed if he'd like to work for us permanently. I told him the pay was five dollars a day. After the way he'd handled everything, I felt like I could trust him.

He readily accepted.

The civil assistance for which we'd hired Mohamed bordered on ridiculous, considering that we had originally been hired to bring down Saddam's government and to destroy his Army. We administered unruly gas stations with thousands of frustrated customers. We helped clean up garbage together. We made sure cooking gas got passed out in the mornings. We set up traffic control points and we guarded water towers. Throughout it all, Ammar was jolly and relaxed. Mohamed on the other hand, started wearing a black knit cap and sunglasses, though I wasn't sure why.

Then, after a month of social disorder in Baghdad, minus any real fighting, the entire 101st Airborne Division received orders to base itself out of Mosul. Our battalion was headed to Tal Afar, a city thirty miles away from the provincial capital.

Rather than find new interpreters in northern Iraq, Battalion allowed us to convince our Baghdad translators to come with us on the journey. We offered to double their pay to ten dollars a day if they would agree to officially become part of the unit. Of the twenty or so translators in the unit, eight decided to make the move with us.

For Ammar, it wasn't a question of *if* he would do it, but of how much stuff he could bring and how much more money he was going to make. Mohamed was a harder sell. He told me that he was going to have to discuss it with his family for a few days. I was disappointed to hear that he was considering not coming because I'd gotten so used to working with him over the past several weeks.

The morning of the day before we left, Mohamed announced as soon as we picked him up for work that he would be joining us on the trip. He seemed reluctant, but resolved to go through with it all the same. I felt that it wasn't any of my business to really probe and find out what the issues were. I just accepted his decision and left it alone. All he asked was that he get to go home that afternoon to gather his things and to have a final dinner with his family that evening.

When we picked him up that night, he was waiting patiently with a single bag outside some shops on a prearranged street corner in Daura. When we pulled over, he approached with some members of his family. I'd never met them before. His father was a balding, middle-aged man, and he was wearing a button-down white shirt and khakis. After I shook his hand, he looked at me with an enthusiastic, yet somehow hesitant smile. Then he said in broken English, "Please take care of our son. We love him very much." It was a terribly direct statement and I could sense the fear and concern.

It's funny—that was the only time a parent of one of my guys ever appealed to me directly to take care of his or her son.

I still hear those words sometimes. It was something about the way he looked at me when he said them. He had so much faith in us, as Americans, that he was willing to give us his son.

Long after I was done with the war, I got an email telling me that American soldiers had shot Mohamed's father behind the wheel of his car when he hadn't stopped at a checkpoint in time. He had lived, but the three bullets that struck him had permanently mangled his left arm. And even though they'd shot Mohamed's father by mistake, the military refused to provide or pay for his medical care.

I often wonder what he thinks of us now.

On the ride back, I wondered what the conversations had been like in Mohamed's house that week. I figured that it was Mohamed's mother who was terrified of letting him go. In the end, they probably decided that just having an income would make it worth it. I gazed at the sky as it faded from purple to black, feeling the wind rushing in through the open window of the moving humvee. Then I looked at Mohamed riding on the bench in the bed of the truck. He seemed content and happy; he seemed at peace with having just joined an army. Maybe he figured he could do some good for his country. The war seemed to be over and the reconstruction looked to be in full swing. I looked ahead at the traffic. Things were looking up. I wondered if this meant that we might be heading home sometime soon.

Then I noticed the traffic stopped ahead.

We snaked our way through the stopped cars and trucks before coming to an intersection. A minivan was turned on its side in the middle of the intersection. Figuring we could help, I stopped the platoon. Walking toward it, I noticed broken glass covering the asphalt like glitter. In the glare of the headlights my long shadow stretched across bodies lying in the street. I looked at the traffic signals and saw that they were as dark as the night itself. No electricity. When I got closer I could hear the music in the tape player of the van still blaring. It fused with the moaning that came from the mouths of the victims.

One of Whipple's guys was first on the scene with an aid bag. More of the guys soon followed. They stepped gingerly over broken glass that was everywhere—glass on which the men from the van were lying.

Four Iraqis had been pulled from the wreckage, but another was still inside, his head crushed between the dash and the pavement. When I stuck my head in the upside down driver's side door, it just looked *wrong*. There was something obviously not right about the way his body looked normal before ending where his neck met the dash and the road. There was just way too little room for a head in there.

The guys worked on the other injured occupants, doing what little they could with what little we had. At the same time, Ammar and Mohamed worked on crowd control, attempting to keep the growing throng of onlookers at bay. All the while the cassette in the van continued to belt out festive tunes in Arabic, giving the scene a twisted quality.

At some point a patrol from the 82nd Airborne happened by and began assisting. With their help we were able to extract the corpse from the van. His face had been torn off completely. I was surprised that his head was still attached. I thought, *That's something good at least.* Someone reached in and ejected the tape. The sudden silence seemed odd. All I could hear were voices, traffic on the periphery, and still more faint moans.

Since our relieving unit was now on site, I decided they could deal with it. I had seen enough.

As we were loading up to leave, I witnessed an ominous sign, though at the time I didn't think much of it. A car turned the corner, driving around the overturned van. It came within inches of Ammar. I watched it, frozen for a second, and then listened as someone inside called something out to him. Without stopping, they drove off.

I walked toward Ammar and asked him what they'd said.

"Oh, it's nothing," he said shaking his head and waving me off in his normal cocky manner. "Some punk just called me a traitor."

We left the next morning out of Baghdad on a day like any other day that spring—sunny and warm. We headed north on Highway One, following the map toward Mosul. Along the way we bypassed Tikrit, probably passing within a mile or two of the still fugitive Saddam Hussein. We traveled past green pastures outside of old Samarra and we drove through the refinery town of Bayji. Journeying north, the landscape began to change. Hills began to rise up and mountains emerged from the haze on the horizon. After a day's drive, we entered the ancient Assyrian capital of Nineveh, now known as Mosul.

There we took a left and drove west into the setting sun. We drove for half an hour until we were less than twenty-five miles from the Syrian border. We drove until we had reached the city of Tal Afar.

9

Northern Iraq
May through October 2003

Tal Afar eventually became a bloody mess. Some of it I was there for, most of it I wasn't. I had been driving the car of fantasy war, playing chicken with the eighteen-wheeler of real war for two years. By the time I lost my nerve and swerved that summer, it was almost too late.

Guys in my battalion lost legs, eyes, and jaws. Three others got killed. They got hit with bullets, grenades, bombs, and RPGs. We killed terrorists and insurgents. In the process we killed civilians. We shot kids. It became pretty standard guerilla war. In a perverse way, it became the war I'd always wanted.

When we got there, Tal Afar was a peaceful city of fifty thousand inhabitants—comprising mostly Turkomen and Kurds, but also a few Arabs. The landscape was hilly and full of scrub brush—and dozens and dozens of archaeological sites. Tal Afar itself is built around the remnants of an Ottoman fortress—that being one of the newer sites.

In the beginning, Croom and I would receive a sector on a map and be told by Captain B. to "find out what they need." What he meant was that we were to drive into the surrounding countryside, go to each individual village with its adobe buildings, thatched roofs, sheep, and chickens, and write down any complaints the local "mukhtar" had. Those could range anywhere from bad roads to no fresh water to "Saddam released all the prisoners before the war and now a murderer lives in our village."

Figuring out a way to fix their predicaments wasn't our problem at that point, however. It was just: meet the mukhtar, write down his complaints, stay for lunch if he insisted, and hand all this "intelligence" over to the battalion headquarters.

We spent the first two weeks working like that. The war was over for us. It had ended over a month earlier in Baghdad during a montage of toppling statues, looting, and explosions. We'd gone back to card playing, magazine reading, and now, cultural immersion.

I was surprised then, when I was told by Captain B. one afternoon to be ready to go on a raid that night with Task Force 20. Task Force 20 was the super-secret amalgamation of what I assumed to be U.S. Army Special Forces, Delta Force, and the CIA. Keeping all the hush-hush task forces straight in my head always took a lot of effort. Task Force 20. Task Force 11. Task Force Dagger. K-Bar. Saber. Task Force Blue. Brown. Hammer. DeathForceKill-9000. They all ran together.

When the Task Force 20 guys actually showed up that night, they appeared to be half of a Special Forces A-team along with a CIA operative who spoke Arabic. The CIA officer was a middle-aged guy with glasses and a New York Yankees baseball cap.

I was upbeat. The mission was to capture the Ten of Diamonds—Saddam's vice president, Taha Yasin Ramadan. He was supposedly nearby, hiding with a gold-toothed bodyguard in an outlying village. My interest in the mission revolved around the soldier's paradox again—I didn't necessarily want to be involved with "Taha's Last Stand," but I had gotten so bored that this was something to break the monotony. It made me feel like I was in the infantry.

But then the Task Force 20 major who was in charge told us that unfortunately, the intel was six days old. *A balloon rockets across the room, discharging all its air from within, and lands flaccidly on the ground at my feet.* With those words—*six days old*—I knew it was futile. I knew that we would end up going through the motions, not capture anybody, and maybe terrify a farmer and his family half to death. Six days when you're chasing fugitives might as well be three years. The pointlessness of the raids was starting to wear on my nerves.

We timed portions of the raid down to the second—something I'd never done before. And it was good practice. Everybody was in position when they were supposed to be. Mohamed was in his disguise—this time a knit cap and a bandana that covered his face. And everything went off without a hitch—except for the fact that Taha wasn't there when we arrived. It came across the radio as, "dry hole."

This surprised no one.

After that I settled back into my job as an infantryman-turned-local water supply officer. We started talking about the war in the past tense whenever we referred to the actual fighting of March and April—as in, "back during the war." Even when vaguely warlike events presented themselves, we conveniently brushed them off or dismissed them as someone else's problem.

One afternoon an orange and white taxi drove up to the front entrance of our compound. I called for Mohamed and then walked out into the fading afternoon light to see what the driver wanted. As we approached the car, the taxi driver opened the rear door closest to us. I stuck my head in while Mohamed talked to the driver.

It was a similar scene to one I'd had to deal with in Baghdad. Crumpled in the back seat was an Iraqi, bleeding from a gunshot wound. He had tears streaming down his face and he was sobbing uncontrollably. He looked terrified. I assumed this was because he believed himself to be running out of blood. I stepped back from the open door.

"Okay, Mohamed. What's the deal? What is this?"

Mohamed responded without taking his eyes off the cab driver. "He says they were attacked by members of the Baath Party . . . and that they were lucky to escape alive." The taxi driver said something and pointed off into the distance. Mohamed continued to translate. "He says they are just up the road . . . only a few kilometers from here."

I looked at Mohamed and smiled, cynically. "Right. That's a new one. I'm sure it's one of Saddam's closest buddies." Insurgency was not yet one of the words in my Iraq war vocabulary. "They're full of shit. We've seen this before. Why don't they go to the hospital in Tal Afar?" I figured they had tried to rob someone and then been thwarted . . . or that it had been something personal—maybe a feud between families.

Mohamed asked the question and then answered me. "He says they want protection."

Protection? The request sounded strange at first, but then I remembered how melodramatic so many of the civilians with whom I'd dealt had been. I rolled my eyes. "Hold on. I'll talk to Captain B." A minute later I came back. Mohamed was still standing next to the taxi conversing with the driver. "Yeah, tell these guys to get the fuck out of here. Go to the hospital in Tal Afar for treatment. We're too busy to deal with this kind of stuff." I glanced into the back seat again and saw that the wounded Iraqi was still bawling.

I wondered why they'd felt the need to bring their problem to us. The war was over. The partisan war we'd all feared in the beginning had never materialized. Issues of violence no longer concerned us. We were more worried about cooking gas distribution, drinking water issues, possible elections, and which coalition country would be the one to relieve us in the next couple of months.

Several days later I was given a one-week notice by Captain B. that I would be leaving Delta Company. He told me that I was being promoted to executive officer and that I'd be going back to Bravo Company to become its second in command. I would return there only two days prior to a new commander taking over for the departing Captain K. That part suited me fine. It would hold the conflicts to a minimum.

I had mixed feelings about the whole thing. I was looking forward to returning to my old company, but I had become comfortable with Sergeant Croom and the Delta guys. I'd fought my second war with them and bonded with them—and

I felt like I was leaving them right in the middle of something we hadn't yet finished as a team. There's never a good time to leave a squad or a platoon or a company. It's just harder in a war—or a sort-of-war. Out of everybody, I think it was Mohamed who took my transfer the hardest.

I spent the first week or so of my new job in a fog. Every aspect of it was foreign to me. Having spent two years in the world of "shoot, move, and communicate," I now had to learn resupply, maintenance cycles, and the art of company movement planning. The new commander, Captain Mike Jones, a West Pointer, had never commanded a company either—so we were learning together.

The whole thing—the war, my job—seemed to be smooth sailing from here on out as far as I was concerned. Northern Iraq was peaceful, unlike the areas nearer Baghdad and Fallujah, where the situation still seemed to be smoldering. I felt like we had lucked out in coming up here.

When the insurgency started in Tal Afar, nobody was killed. There was neither a wounded soldier nor a shot fired. When it happened, we weren't even sure if we'd actually been attacked. The event was at the same time insidious and laughable—and it signaled the spread of the cancerous insurgency to northwest Iraq.

I had been inside the TOC talking to Phil and another soldier when I decided to rack out for the evening in Bravo Company's barracks building next door. I walked outside the open door in the rear of the TOC wearing only desert camouflage bottoms, sandals, and a brown t-shirt . There was a slight breeze blowing that made the hot night bearable. I first stepped toward the barracks building, but then remembered that I wanted to take a leak before heading off to bed.

The piss tubes were located at the rear of the property, not fifty feet away from the door through which I'd just walked. They backed up to the fortified, sand-filled barrier that marked the northern edge of our headquarters. I walked that direction, carefully stepping over the puddles of water left by our big metal camouflaged water buffalo. I reached the tubes, picked out the most sanitary-looking one, unbuttoned, and conducted my business. The operation went as planned.

I shook it off, buttoned back up, and turned to head back to my waiting cot. I'd walked about thirty feet when a blast shattered the evening calm. It came from the alleyway behind the barriers, on the other side of the piss tubes—not twenty feet from where I'd been standing. I wondered if I was just a magnet for random explosives.

For a second I stood there, confused. *Does this concern me?* I looked at the barrier wall, scanning for smoke or a breach, listening for voices or a car. But in the darkness I couldn't see anything. And there was only silence. The thought of an attack didn't even register. That was out of the question. Our war had ended two months earlier, sometime in April. Of course there was some harassment taking place in the newly christened Sunni Triangle, but that wasn't anywhere close to us. Our main problems were civil in nature—not guerilla.

From inside the TOC I heard a, "What the fuck was that?"

Then something changed inside my head. I don't know what and I don't know why, but it did. It just didn't *feel* right anymore. I turned and hurried back to the building. Before I got there, guys were already coming out to see what all the racket had been about. I walked back to the CP near my room. Some guys were putting on boots; others were just sitting on the edges of their cots looking inconvenienced by the mystery noise. Nobody knew what to do. We debated whether you could counterattack a mystery noise and couldn't come up with anything.

Word was passed to gear up into full battle rattle, and we decided to dispatch a squad to go check out the perimeter of the headquarters. Those of us now indoors largely ignored the first order, but we did send a squad to investigate.

Meanwhile, the platoon leaders and I wagered on what the result would be. I didn't have any clue as to what it could have been, but I wasn't yet convinced that it was a *real* attack. Things had just been too *peaceful* in Tal Afar for the last eight weeks.

The next morning I was told that somebody had set two barrels against the back wall of our compound. In the bottoms they had placed old artillery shells. And on top they had placed wood and trash. They lit the barrels on fire, in the hopes that when the fire reached the bottom the shells would explode.

It was good initiative, but bad judgment on their part. Unfortunately for the insurgent, only one of the rounds detonated, causing a minor fire on the barrier wall. The effort had been paltry at best, showing distinct signs of amateurism. Placing explosives at the base of a "blast wall" usually runs contrary to conventional wisdom in guerilla warfare. You're supposed to hit the weak points, not the blast walls.

But that's not the point. The bottom line was that the peace forged after the fall of Baghdad—the peace in which we'd lived for the last two months in Tal Afar—had just ended. With a muffled boom and nothing else, it had ended. By the hands of some clumsy amateur, it had simply ceased being. Unknown to us, we had been facing a dam all along—a dam that had now cracked and sprung a leak. Behind it was a deluge of terrorists and insurgents, IEDs, and RPGs.

I am in the mountains, standing next to Sergeant Collins. The Shah-e-Kot Valley, still smoking after an endless week of pounding, stretches out before us. It is a clear dusk and now that the sun has dropped behind the ridge to the west, we can each see our own breath. A B-52, thousands of feet above us, is flying in our direction. Without taking his eyes off of the plane, Collins says, "Wouldn't it be fucked up if he dropped his payload right now?"

"Yeah, it would," I say. "Hey, wait a sec. . .What is . . ."

A dozen little pale dots are now visible below the flying aircraft. Slowly, they fall behind it—drifting in our direction. He has dropped his payload of dumb bombs. For a second I want to panic. I realize that if I could run at this altitude, there's no way I could outrun such a number of bombs. If they are going to hit our position, they will hit it, and we will be vaporized. Even if the pilot has made a mistake, even if he realizes it, there's nothing he can do to call them back. It has already happened to us once.

Reading my mind, Sergeant Collins, eyes still glued to the sky, says, "That's the kind of shit you can't run from."

The bombs gradually float directly over us, getting bigger by the second. Their trajectory takes them onto the south side of the mountain next to us, where they impact with not-too-distant thuds.

I often dream of falling bombs. Sometimes they're of things that really happened, and I'm back in the valley. Other times they're not, and strange, far away cannons are launching screaming orange fireballs in my direction. Either way, it's the same feeling of helplessness and terror. In neither dream can I escape.

In Iraq, these were replayed weekly like old film reels through my head at night. And when it wasn't falling bombs it was mountain shootouts. When it wasn't combat, it was Nikki.

I can't remember now what I was dreaming about at half past eleven on the night of July 19. It could have been any of the three.

I opened my eyes and turned my head toward the door of the room. I was still half asleep. In the doorway I could see a sil-houette against the lit hallway. I recognized it as Specialist Kuykendall, Captain Jones' RTO. Not sure if I was still dream-ing, I wondered what he was doing standing there. Then I real-ized he must have awakened me. He'd probably been standing there saying my name. I reached up to my ears and pulled out a pair of now silent headphones.

"What . . ." I paused and cleared my throat. "What's up, man? What do you need?" I asked him.

He said something about a shooting, but whatever he said didn't really strike me as something that was important to me.

Still groggy and unmoved from my cot, I said, "Anybody hurt? Was it any of our guys?" I only had one eye open.

He said he didn't know about casualties but that it was def-initely not Bravo Company.

I propped myself up on an elbow. "Kuykendall, do I need to get up for this?" I felt like I was about to pass right back out. I was vaguely thinking that this was most likely gunfire that didn't concern me.

He said he didn't think so. He said he was just passing along chatter he'd heard on the radio and thought maybe I should know about it since Captain Jones was gone for the evening.

"Thanks, man," I said. "Come wake me up again if this turns into a big deal or something."

He said he would, no problem.

I passed into unconsciousness.

"Sir, you need to wake up. Lieutenant Friedman . . . Sir, you awake?"

It was Kuykendall's voice again. I opened my eyes. I felt like I'd just closed them a second earlier. I looked at my watch. Twenty minutes had passed since he'd come around the first time. I propped myself up on my elbow again, squinting into the light that came from the hallway. "Yeah, what's up, man?"

"Sir, you need to get up. The commander's on his way back here. Battalion's getting spun up . . . there was an attack on the mortar platoon. . . ."

I stopped him. I knew from the sound of his voice that we were in trouble. I was already swinging my legs out of the cot and putting my boots on. "Kuykendall," I said, trying to find his eyes somewhere on the silhouette that stood in the doorframe, "how bad is it?"

He didn't hesitate. "Two dead, sir. One wounded."

Before the words were out of his mouth my stomach had already dropped. I threw my head back and looked at the ceiling. I brought it back down and rubbed my eyes with the palms of my hands. "Be there in a second," I said.

For twenty seconds I sat there on the edge of my cot, letting the fact sink in that after nearly two years of war, our luck had

finally run out. The barrel-bomb at the TOC had been our luck
sputtering. Now it was gone.

I had been sleeping in the master bedroom of an oil company's
guesthouse at Ayn Zalah. We had temporarily relocated the
company CP to this small but upscale village that sat among a
group of hills forty miles northeast of Tal Afar. From the high
ground at Ayn Zalah, there is a spectacular view of the lake
caused by the damming of the Tigris. On clearer days there,
you can see through the summer haze and into the mountains
of Turkey. And at night you can look out across the water and
view the tiny city lights of the Kurdish city of Dohuk.

I was sharing a room with Captain Jones, but he had been
spending the night with Sergeant Collins and the guys in my old
platoon. They were just over a mile away at a compound near the
southern edge of the village. Now he was en route back to the
guesthouse with Mike Bandzwolek, the lieutenant to whom I'd
given over command of the platoon before the deployment.

I walked into the dining room where we had the radios set
up. It was also where we had meetings. I sat down, half asleep
and half in shock, and just stared at the table in front of me.
Kuykendall told me that the other platoon leaders had been
called and were on their way here.

At that moment 2nd Lieutenant Ted P.* swung open the
screen door at the front of the building, letting it slam behind
him on his way in. He ambled over to the dining room table
and plopped down at my left elbow. He was a big guy and had
only joined the battalion in Baghdad. I noticed he had red
sleep lines on the right side of his face.

* Name abbreviated for security purposes.

He looked at me, raised his eyebrows, and smiled. "What's up, man? What the fuck am I over here for?"

He had no idea. I looked him in the eye and saw that he was still grinning. For the moment, Ted was innocent. He had a degree in music, and I was pretty sure Ted had never killed a mammal. To my knowledge, the most trauma Ted had experienced was being "raped" by an older woman he'd brought home from a bar one night in college. There were a couple of other guys in the room and I could feel them stop moving.

"Two KIA. Friendly. One wounded," I stated flatly. "I don't know anything else."

Ted looked at me, his grin widening. Then he glanced at someone who was standing on the other side of the table. He looked like he thought we were playing a joke on him. "Yeah, right. Whatever," he quipped. "Seriously, why am I not still asleep?" The war wasn't *real* yet for Ted.

I looked him directly in the eye again. For some reason I had the strange urge to laugh. Nerves. I'd never before announced a death to someone—at least not one that mattered like this did, anyway. I stifled the smirk and kept a straight face. When I spoke, I spoke softly and awkwardly. "No man, I'm serious. We got two dead. Commander's on his way back with Mike."

Ted's eyes doubled in size. He grinned again in reflex, except this time he looked nauseous. He said, "Who was it?"

I just shrugged. "Don't know yet."

When Captain Jones burst in with Bandzwolek behind him, they strode directly to our table and sat down. We waited in an awkward silence for 3rd Platoon's leader. He was coming from the town of Zumar, five miles away. It seemed like hours—the fidgeting and the glances and the nervous exhalations. Finally, he walked through the screen door carrying his green bound notebook.

Then we learned details.

Justin Garvey and Jason Jordan. I didn't know either of them personally. I only knew their faces and names—from passing them in the upstairs hallway at Fort Campbell to sharing time in the chow hall line in Kuwait to any other number of places. Five minutes earlier, they had just been two sergeants in the mortar platoon. Now, all around the battalion, their names were being seared into our collective memory. It's like that the first time you're given the names of people killed in your unit. You get their names permanently branded onto your mind.

Someone had fired RPGs at the mortar section's convoy at nearly the same time as they hit the TOC in Tal Afar. The TOC took only a minor hit from two RPG rounds that took out a chunk from the outer wall, shredded a few cots, and caused one minor injury. The other half of the coordinated attack had turned out differently.

The mortar platoon had been conducting a traffic control point that evening, stopping and searching cars, looking for anything out of the ordinary. They had run the traffic stop several miles east of Tal Afar. When they'd finished they had driven several humvees back in the direction of town. They were following the main road that links Tal Afar with Mosul, just after eleven o'clock at night. As they passed through the village of Abu Mariyah, a single RPG round struck the lead vehicle containing Garvey, Jordan, and a sergeant named Doug Norman, a former Bravo guy I knew well. It was a one in a hundred shot, hitting the front windshield and killing the two sergeants instantly. Norman was thrown out of the bed of the truck with shrapnel embedded in both of his legs. In a burst of adrenaline he was able to get up, recover his machine gun, and return fire.

He emptied an entire drum of bullets into the darkness, hitting absolutely nothing.

Less than an hour after the initial attack, the response plan didn't amount to much. All we knew was that the bulk of the battalion—a unit of six hundred men spread over six hundred square miles—was going to converge on the village of Abu Mariyah before the sun came up.

It sounded to me like it had the potential to get ugly. It sounded as if we were getting ready to sweep through the village like a tornado.

I was partly disturbed at the idea. Not because I didn't think we should show up there that night, but because, to me, it had all the hallmarks of the invasion of Iraq—a poorly thought out, hasty plan that ends in far more lives being lost and property being destroyed than is really necessary. And I knew for a fact that there were lots of women, children, old people, dogs, goats, chickens, and mules in Abu Mariyah. The village itself was constructed of mud, straw, and perhaps a few cinder blocks. And now they were going to face one of the single most deadly military units in the world—a unit that was going to light upon them in the biblical sense, probably in a blind rage.

I thought of the lone horse in Anaconda and then to that first day in Baghdad—to the girl and the two men who thought we were going to execute them. I remembered how they had had nothing to do with the reason why I was in Iraq. And I remembered how horrible that made me feel. This coming altercation was going to be far worse for everyone on both sides.

On the other hand, I couldn't stop thinking about how we had been *violated* as a unit. I couldn't stop thinking about how two guys had just been murdered—and how their families didn't even know it yet. That part of me was ready to burn the entire place to the ground.

We began staging in the darkness outside of the guesthouses. A single streetlamp lit the area. I could see 2nd Platoon's squad leaders going through pre-combat checks with their guys. Near me, Captain Jones stayed glued to his radio's hand mike, taking instructions.

Two of Bravo's three Kurdish translators were conversing in Arabic next to a humvee. Like Ammar and Mohamed, Hameed and Waseem had come with the battalion from Baghdad.

Hameed was the crazy one. After returning to Bravo Company, I'd learned immediately that if the Iraqi military was ever going to get back on its feet, he should be in charge at some level. Just from looking at the friendly smile plastered on the balding guy's face, you would never have believed that Hameed had been an Iraqi Special Forces commando during the Iran-Iraq War of the 1980s.

Always wearing a baseball cap to block the harsh Iraqi sun, Hameed used to recount his war stories for the guys. Sometimes he would compare them to this war. "Yah, that war was much, much different than this one," he'd say. "In that time you were always having to jump around like a monkey to get away from bullets . . . like this." He'd then hop back and forth from one foot to the other.

His experience in the Army, along with his being of Kurdish descent, had made him virulently anti-Saddam. He was also equally as violent when it came to his pro-American leanings. Hameed wasn't afraid to hit or threaten to kill Iraqis who gave us a hard time. He was the most proactive translator I'd ever seen—always trying to get tips from the populace to help out the Americans. And Hameed feared no one.

Waseem was Hameed's opposite. He was the reserved and sincere one—and not nearly as reactionary as Hameed. Waseem had been a track and field champion until he was barred from the 1988 Olympics simply for the fact that he was Kurdish. There were always a lot of guys like that who joined the unit— guys who had been fucked with by Saddam's thugs.

Considering what had just happened, there didn't seem to be a lot of talking between soldiers. For one thing, except for the few who had been patrolling or on guard, everyone had just woken up. On top of that, nothing like this had ever happened to us. It hadn't yet set in that the Battalion had just endured a successful surprise attack—or that we'd taken casualties while exacting none in return. It had that 9/11-like quality to it, where you've been slapped in the face so hard that the reality and gravity of the situation isn't really registering. We had been numbed by so much quasi-combat for two years, that now, faced with the real thing, it had an almost anticlimactic air about it.

As I got closer and closer to launching Bravo Company into the village of Abu Mariyah, I began to feel nothing—for myself, for Jordan and Garvey, or for the inhabitants, whether they were innocent or guilty. I just wanted to get it over with.

Then, with trucks rumbling and troops loaded, I was told that the operation had been stopped indefinitely. Brigade, sensing a slaughter I presume, ordered the battalion to cease with the operation. Again, I was caught in the middle. I was incensed that the brigade commander would pull the plug on our right to avenge our dead. But at the same time, I could sense that before daylight we would be knee deep in a blood-bath. It hadn't been ordered; there was just a feeling of reck-lessness and reprisal attached to every aspect of the plan I'd heard. And I could just see it in the looks on guys' faces, their attitudes, their comments. As emotionally detached as every-one seemed to be, it could have been bloody. Expressionless robots are capable of inflicting the most damage.

As guys were dismounting from the trucks, I found Captain Jones. He was still geared up and standing near his humvee. I said, "What the fuck is this? What are we gonna do now?" I felt like we had to do something. And while I wasn't too keen on killing civilians, the idea of doing nothing in the face of a fatal attack was simply wrong.

He just looked at me and shrugged. Then he said, "I guess we go back to bed."

My men are not expendable. And I don't do this kind of work.

Lying on my cot that night, I hated. It was a new thing for me. It had been building each day that no weapons of mass destruction were found—and now it was coming to a head. I had never hated before—not like this. I had never hated the enemy, nor had I ever feared the enemy. I was always emotionally neutral when it came to that. I had feared dying, but never the enemy. Now still, I did not hate whoever had been behind the RPG. You go to a war—these things happen. I knew that. But you go to an unnecessary war and it happens—well that's completely different.

I had always wanted to fight. But I never wanted any part of something like this. I was a professional soldier. I wanted to believe in my work. Instead, I was watching as politicians with no military experience hijacked the Army. I was a public servant, not a lackey. Lying on my cot, I came to the point that many people reach in a situation where they stop what they're doing and say, "Wait a second. This is bullshit. This isn't right." Two guys in our battalion were dead, two families ruined. And try as I might, I couldn't figure out what the purpose of that was.

Things that had been welling up inside me all summer suddenly exploded in my head like a dozen Roman candles. I hated the president for his ignorance. I hated Donald Rumsfeld for his appalling arrogance and his lack of judgment. I hated their agenda. I hated Colin Powell for abandoning the Army—for not taking care of his soldiers—when he could have done something to stop these people. I hated them because the Army had seen this insurgency coming. I hated them because they didn't listen to the people who told them this was a bad plan. I hated them because now, it meant that my guys could be next. It meant that I could be next. And I didn't want to die like this—not in a confusing mishmash of ideologies, purposes, and bullets.

I felt like we had been taken advantage of. We were professionals sent on a wild goose chase using a half-baked plan for political reasons. Lying there restlessly, I was reminded of a Schwarzenegger line in one of his movies—when, after being used and lied to, his muscle-bound character had expressed perfectly what was now on my mind: *My men are not expendable. And I don't do this kind of work.*

I longed for the clarity of purpose we'd had in Afghanistan.

It is Tuesday, September 11. Nikki and I are standing next to each other in her living room, staring at the screen. President Bush is in a dimly lit room making a speech to the American people. He is in a bunker at Barksdale Air Force Base, not three miles from where we are standing. He seems nervous and anxious—maybe even a bit awkward since he realizes that the entire nation is watching him. But he also seems resolute. It is that sense that makes me feel at least okay about how this will be handled.

We want to get out of the house, so we decide to go get lunch somewhere. A mile down the road, Nikki says she wants Applebee's. I'm not at all surprised. It's comfort food for her. Inside, we sit at one of the high tables. Nikki is already disgusted and doesn't want to watch any more news, so I face the television. Shortly after the server takes our order, I say, "Nikki, turn around. Look at that. People are jumping out of the building. I didn't see that earlier. Did you?"

So we dealt with it, I thought, staring at the ceiling. *We fixed a very significant part of the problem. Why this now?* In Afghanistan I'd seen captured Pakistanis, Saudis, Yemenis, Jordanians, Kuwaitis, and Chechens, but I'd never heard of a single Iraqi even being in Afghanistan. *We had been hot on the trail. Why Iraq? We* know *they're in western Pakistan. We* know *they're in Saudi Arabia.* That we had invaded Iraq with all these other threats swirling around us was beginning to seem more and more preposterous to me.

Whether we had come to prevent the spread of weapons of mass destruction or to remove an evil dictator, the end result was that we had created an increasingly complex insurgency. And in defining this insurgency, there were those who wanted to pin the attacks on thousands of mysterious al Qaeda terrorists, when in reality most of them were the work of regular run-of-the-mill insurgents.

It was as if no one had read a book on resistance movements and insurgencies—or seen the movie *Red Dawn*. It goes like this in every insurgency: There are a few fighters who have a real political agenda for killing both the invaders and those who would build a new government; there are a few foreign zealots, a few religious zealots, a few more foreign religious zealots, and then there are the rest of them—the overwhelming majority of whom are young, impressionable, male, unemployed, bored, and pissed about, among other things, the fact that their uncle was killed in an air strike or their cousin was killed at a traffic control point for not stopping soon enough. Without this last group there would be no insurgency. The population just wouldn't support it in a place like Iraq. Maybe in Afghanistan, but not in Iraq.

You have to put yourself in their shoes. If a foreign country invaded the United States, it wouldn't matter if they came handing out hundred dollar bills and a cure for AIDS. If they fucked over one family in an American neighborhood, a resistance would form. It doesn't make it right—it just makes it reality.

And with these types of insurgencies, the longer you stay there the worse it gets. On a long-enough timeline, an occupying force will eventually piss off everyone. That's just what happens, even when you come with the best of intentions.

I could still hear the words of Colonel Ahuja bouncing around in my head—words spoken months earlier in the Kuwaiti desert: *I think there's always gonna be that guy who's out to fight for his country no matter what. He doesn't care about the politics. He just knows that we're invading* his *country. And he knows he's gonna to do everything in his power to stop us.*

I didn't know who'd killed Jordan and Garvey. Maybe it had been foreign jihadists or Wahabbi fundamentalists. Maybe it had been a citizen of Tal Afar who'd felt slighted by us for some reason. It didn't matter to me. All I could think of was that we should have kept up the fight against the terrorists in their own lairs—and not brought our war to the streets of Iraq. Taking the fight here, I thought, with no preparation for what had to be a complicated aftermath, was shortsighted and reckless. Committing soldiers' lives without having first come up with a coherent plan, I thought, was criminal.

Now I could see that the victory we had achieved in the aftermath of 9/11, all of the good will that we as a nation had garnered, was slowly going to be ground away in the streets of Iraq.

It wasn't supposed to happen this way. We were young. We were invincible. We were the good guys. Or so we had thought.

When Garvey and Jordan were killed, it sent a shockwave through the battalion and the community. Iraqis brought flowers and laid them at the front gate of the TOC. The caretaker of the oil company village at Ayn Zalah came around the next afternoon to offer his condolences on behalf of the Iraqis that lived up there by the lake. The response by the people was somewhat of a surprise to me, but after I thought about it, I could see that it shouldn't have been. We had been working with them on the reconstruction for two months and had earned their trust. Now, in a way, the citizens of Tal Afar and its surrounding communities seemed almost embarrassed at the way their "guests" had been treated.

During the time after the attack we moped. I had always thought that when a soldier from my unit died in combat it would come with a sense of inevitability—a sense that that kind of thing was *supposed* to happen. Being an infantryman, I thought it would be not only normal, but also easy to deal with. I had seen too many fucking movies.

The reality was a slap in the face. The sense of loss and failure was palpable across the unit, the fear of dying rekindled. We had become so complacent after a long string of anticlimaxes. But now the landscape had changed. Now everything was suspect. From that point on, every time I left the perimeter, I would see an insurgent behind every bend in the road; in every ditch, a possible ambush point.

It turned everything sour. Driving around rural northern Iraq every day, I was used to seeing the shepherds herding their sheep in the open fields. The thing was, they always wore red turbans wrapped around their faces the way you always see Palestinian terrorists wear them in videos and on posters. In the beginning, it was disconcerting to see that every day. The media had conditioned my brain to think terrorist whenever I saw the red mask, not shepherd. But sitting on their donkeys, the teenagers underneath the red masks always waved at us when we drove by. They seemed happy every time one of us waved back to them. Seeing people who looked the way I had been trained to think terrorists looked, and having them wave at me, taught me something about perception and reality.

That progress was ruined by the attack. Whether or not anything else ever happened again in Tal Afar, the trust that we had built within the community during those two months was gone. Now, in the fight-or-flight part of my brain, they were terrorists again. If it came down to it, and I was put in a bad situation, those who looked the way I thought terrorists looked would not get the benefit of the doubt.

I was too afraid of dying.

Driving outside the wire on the day after Jordan and Garvey were killed, nothing had changed from the time the ramp had lowered in Operation Anaconda—except the landscape. The nausea in the pit of my stomach—the fear itself—had not dimmed one bit. It had just been on hiatus. It was back now and I could not subdue the intensity of the feeling that death could come in the next few minutes. In my case it always seemed to manifest itself as an external coolness that masked an internal panic. I was convinced that if I were hit, there would be no warning—I would simply be snuffed out. I knew it would be complete, and had no doubt in my mind that I would return to the state in which I had been before my birth—a state of oblivion. I realized that everything taught to me while growing up was in fact nonsense—nonsense devised to assist people in coping with death. I now realized—I knew, in fact—that if I were killed, I would cease to exist. This sentiment never waned when death was near. Not once.

Guerilla warfare is perhaps the most psychologically damaging to soldiers. It's what made Vietnam so bad. It is much easier for the human mind to deal with the extreme violence of something like Iwo Jima or Normandy. There, the soldier knew when he would have to fight and when he wouldn't. He knew when it would start and when it was over. His mind could compartmentalize. In combat, he was afraid. When it was over, he no longer had to be afraid. Those soldiers had front lines. In Iraq, the soldiers live in a constant state of fear, because there is no "battlefield." They are always being targeted, whether it's driving around in a city, standing in a chow line on base, or sleeping in their racks. There is no safe place in Iraq. Over the course of months, this constant medium-level stress, with a few spikes to higher levels, can wreak havoc on the mind. And when men in your unit start dying at the hands of shadowy assailants, even if it's only two of them, the unit is basically traumatized by the fear of the unknown. You realize that you are always being watched.

During this time, my window in which to decide whether or not to stay in the Army was quickly closing. I had to choose. I could either leave Iraq in the middle of October or stay in the Army for at least another two years, risking further stop-losses.

I could no longer justify continuing to push my luck. I thought about my family. An irrational part of me even wanted to try working things out with Nikki even though I knew she'd moved on. I loved the Army, but I could hear Collins' voice inside my head: *A man's got to know his limitations.*

I'd wanted out before, but this—this was it. I guess I just didn't have the stomach for it anymore. Maybe the stupidity of the war in the broadest sense just kind of got to me. Or maybe the politics. Maybe it was just that the whole thing had turned out to be something other than what I'd thought it would be. I don't know. I did know, however, that my fun meter was pegged.

And I'd never felt guiltier.

As July turned to August, and August to September, the insurgency began rapidly metastasizing in areas further south. By the middle of September, the roadside bomb made its first appearance in northern Iraq, wounding two guys I knew in Delta Company. When I was first told they had been hit with an IED on the way to the Mosul Dam, I wasn't sure I even knew what the acronym stood for. A week later a Brigade convoy got ambushed on the road into Mosul. The whirlpool had begun slowly sucking us in.

As September drew to a close, I was preparing to leave. I went to Delta Company's compound on an October afternoon in order to say goodbye to Sergeant Croom and the guys.

Half of them were out on a patrol when I got there, including Croom. And Mohamed was on a four-day vacation in Baghdad. I had his email address, but it still kind of disappointed me that I wouldn't get to say goodbye in person. I did find Ammar, however. He couldn't wait to see me. He wanted to show me what he'd bought with all the money he'd earned translating since April. We walked out front where several vehicles were parked. One of them was Ammar's new car. He wanted to show it to me, inside and out. While he was doing that, he told me of how on his way back to Tal Afar from Baghdad, he'd accidentally run an American checkpoint in Mosul and almost gotten killed for it. We took some pictures of each other standing by the car and then walked over to the kebab stand and bought French fries to take back to his room.

The sandbags in his bedroom window weren't there when I had lived in the same building. With no more natural light shining in, the room he shared with Croom was given a weak, eerie glow by a single fluorescent lamp. Slathering his fries in ketchup, Ammar asked if I wanted to see a movie. I told him sure, as long as it was a good one. He popped some cheesy 1960s Western into his new DVD player.

After a few minutes, he looked at me with a ketchup-covered French fry in hand and said, "Isn't this movie great?"

When Croom finally returned, I didn't have much time left. We talked about me leaving the Army, and he said that if he were in my position, he'd do the same thing. As things were, Croom was only two years from retirement, so he was going to try to make it. We rechecked our email and phone numbers for when he got back to the States, and that was it.

I walked down to the Delta Company supply sergeant and turned in my ammunition and magazines.

I went back to Bravo Company in Tal Afar next. After meetings with the battalion XO and the battalion commander, there would be nothing left to do but wait for my ride down to the airfield. Once there, I was to simply wait a few more days for another ride—this one to Mosul. From there, I would fly to Kuwait—and then home.

I was no longer Bravo Company's XO and I was no longer responsible for anything but the weapon I held in my hand. My only job now was to turn it in to Specialist Shields, Bravo's armorer. It was the strangest feeling I've ever had. A war was going on around me, a war that I had been a part of from the beginning. It had been two years and twenty days since my dad woke me that morning while I was on leave and told me we were under attack. Now, for the first time since September 11, I had nowhere to be, nothing to do.

I had always envisioned that when I quit soldiering the final "turning in" of my weapon would be somewhat ceremonial and somber. Now I figured that I would just give it a good brushing and hand it to Shields in the morning. That would seal the deal. Where I thought there would be nostalgia and a bit of sadness, there was only the overwhelming desire to leave as quickly as I could.

By the time I got out of my meeting with the XO, it was nearly eleven o'clock at night. I walked into Bravo Company's TV room and sat down next to Captain Jones. He was ready for bed, wearing a brown t-shirt, PT shorts, and flip-flops. Fox News was on, and one of the hosts was trying to make a witty comment about the weather.

First Platoon was supposed to be back to pick me up in the next fifteen minutes. They'd waited around for me, but when the battalion commander had delayed our talk by an hour, their newest Lieutenant, Mike Gerasimus, decided to go ahead with their patrol for the evening. Gerasimus was another former West Pointer who had only recently taken over the platoon from Bandzwolek.

For ten minutes Jones and I sat there making small talk. Specialist Peter O'Brien, his days of cricket formations and droning long behind him, came in for a minute and stared at the screen, completely uninterested, before leaving. At five minutes to eleven, O'Brien stuck his head in and said they were back. I looked up from the TV and noticed I could hear the humvees rumbling outside the back door. I stood up, and after a final handshake with Captain Jones, threw on my vest, grabbed my stuff, and walked out to meet my old platoon.

They were rolling with four trucks. Lieutenant Gerasimas was in the lead truck and Sergeant Collins was in the second. I walked up to Gerasimas, thanked him for the ride, and then asked if he cared which truck I rode in.

"Nah, you can jump in here with me if you want," he said.

I looked in the bed of the truck. Staring back at me were Sergeant Chad Corn, one of my Anaconda vets, Specialist Jason Krogh, Pfc. Lance Lawrence, and Waseem, the hammer-thrower from Baghdad. I noticed Waseem was now wearing a vest with plates. Up front, I could see Private Jason Gasko in the driver's seat.

I felt naked with no ammo. I also felt like dead weight. I figured I had to ask for some, if only to make myself feel better. I reached down into the cab and tapped Gerasimas on the shoulder. "Hey, can you spare some ammo?"

"Sure man, how much you want?" he asked.

"I think one mag oughta do. I've gone through two wars without firing a shot. I think this mag'll last me to the airfield."

Gerasimas just chuckled as he handed me the fully loaded thirty-round magazine. I inserted it into my M4 and charged the handle, chambering a round.

The road directly in front of the headquarters had been blocked off at night since the attack of July 19, so we headed around the block, into the neighborhood directly west of the TOC. As we drove, I couldn't help but think that this was the last time I would ever ride in a tactical situation with an infantry platoon.

Sitting directly behind Gasko as he drove, I looked at the guys around me in the orange glow of passing streetlights. Lawrence was the new guy—as XO, I had picked him up at the TOC only two months ago. He had been fresh off the plane and looked like he was about eighteen years old. Now he was standing right beside me, manning the mounted SAW. Across from me were Waseem and Krogh. Waseem looked as stoic as usual, and Krogh looked only marginally more anxious. Sitting beside me was the newly promoted Sergeant Corn. We hadn't been sitting there long when Corn and I started in on each other with the sarcastic verbal barbs we'd been exchanging for two years. Somewhere in there, we mentioned that this would be our last ride together.

As we drove the long way around the block, I stared at the dilapidated buildings we passed. I noticed the sheet metal walls, the open sewers, and the general grime that covered the city. As usual, there were groups of young men hanging out late on the street corners and in the fronts of shops. I could see a few drinking tea. Only a couple of more days and I would be home, leaving all this in the past.

We approached a four-way intersection and Gasko eased onto the brake as the truck neared the stop sign. The truck rocked back gently as he brought it to a complete stop. Out of the corner of my eye I saw another car pull up to the intersection, perpendicular to us. It was a blue Volkswagen Passat, identical to about a thousand other cars in Tal Afar.

The driver of the Passat rolled to a halt. In our headlights I could see the driver, a passenger, and maybe more people in the back. I couldn't tell. Nor did I care at the moment. But then I saw the driver and the front seat passenger look at us. Immediately, the driver floored it, and blew past us from left to right. In my mind, it registered as "noticeable," and maybe "a little weird," but not dangerous. For a split second, I thought maybe I was the only one that even noticed it. I thought maybe the guy was in a hurry—and that maybe the look they gave us was simply my imagination.

I was wrong. Everybody saw the same thing. Before the blue car had even cleared the intersection, I heard Waseem say in his heavily accented, deep, monotone voice, "Something is not right."

Gerasimas looked at Gasko and yelled, "Follow 'em! Go! Go! Go!"

At this moment of action, I couldn't help but think of other things. I realized that I needed to get a good night's rest and it was already late. Now we were going to chase some guys around Tal Afar. I knew the end of the story already: We would chase them. They would pull over. We would pull the occupants out of the car. We would kick them around for trying to evade us. We would find a couple of AK-47s in the trunk—if we were lucky. Or maybe the driver would just be drunk. No laws against that here. If there were weapons, we'd confiscate them and throw them in the bed of our humvee. And finally, depending on how suspicious the guys looked, we'd determine whether or not to put bags on their heads and take them in for questioning. All in all, I figured that it would take at least an hour to sort through the whole thing. It was another instance that reeked of wasted time just like every other raid or traffic control point I'd managed while in Iraq. I didn't say anything, but I hoped that we would either lose them in traffic or Gerasimas would call it off. I didn't think two AK-47s were worth my time.

Gasko hit the gas and swerved onto the main road. Already there were cars between the Passat and us. Gasko accelerated and started to snake his way through the nighttime traffic. The Passat was easy to follow, as it had a broken rear taillight. *This might not be so bad,* I thought. *We'll catch up to him in a second. We'll flag him down. He'll play stupid. He'll pull over. We may be able to wrap this thing up in twenty minutes.*

Half a second after the thought crossed my mind that this could possibly end quickly, I noticed that the Passat was weaving through traffic as well. And not only that, but he was accelerating. It didn't take very long for me to figure out what this implied. *Jeeesus.* He had something in the car worth the risk of dodging cars and people at high speed.

Gasko started laying on the horn, hitting it first in short bursts, and then in five- to ten-second ones. The Iraqis were slow to get out of the way. American soldiers were known throughout the country for muscling their way through traffic at the expense of the Iraqis. Subsequently, the Iraqis had grown weary of it over the months and were now in no mood to hurry. The Passat was having the same problem.

As we sped in and out of traffic, Gerasimas got a call on the radio: The second humvee, the one with Sergeant Collins, was having trouble keeping up the pace. There was something wrong with the engine, the accelerator, or both. I couldn't make out most of the conversation from the bed of the truck, but I did hear a "Fucking catch up!" from the front seat. The problem was that with the traffic congestion, the other two humvees couldn't get around the second one, and we were thus losing all three. As we blew through traffic, I imagined the earful that Collins' driver was currently withstanding. In an unspoken decision, Gerasimas had decided that we couldn't wait.

The Passat turned off the main road and drove into a neighborhood. Shops lined the street and many were still open. In the blur this chase was quickly becoming, I could see people standing on the side of the road watching. Seeing Americans speed through your neighborhood was nothing new, but this late at night, in hot pursuit of an Iraqi car was something to gawk at.

I began to think we actually might *not* catch the Passat. By then though, my attitude had improved somewhat. If for no other reason, I at least wanted to see what was in the car that was so important that they felt the need to set us on a high-speed chase. I was suddenly a bit disappointed that they might get away.

The road was bumpy and we were driving fast, so I couldn't see much of anything clearly. But within a few seconds I could tell that the Passat was slowing down. Then it turned left at a break in the median, making a U-turn. As we made ground, no one spoke.

The car cleared the turn and started back in our direction just as we reached the cut in the median. As we passed them, I saw the driver, the passenger, and at least one other person in the back seat. Due to its lack of horsepower, the Volkswagen didn't accelerate out of the turn nearly as fast as the humvee and that allowed us to close within fifty feet of it.

At the first side street, he took a hard right, nearly flipping the light car. Again, we gained more ground on the turn, coming to within thirty feet of the little blue car. As the road became bumpier, we started getting jostled around. Trying to balance myself, I found it harder and harder to see clearly with only headlights and intermittent streetlights. The gap was only twenty-five feet between the speeding car and us.

I was aiming my M4 over the top of the cab of the humvee, resting my elbows on the roof for support, when I saw movement in the back seat of the Passat. Due to the bobbing and the speed, I couldn't really tell what they were doing, but I had an idea that they were up to no good. I held my aim as steadily as possible, no longer concerned about my cot at the airfield.

And then they made their decision.

From behind Waseem, Krogh screamed, "He's gotta gun! He's gotta gun!"

I could see movement, but no gun. My mind was racing and I thought maybe Krogh had made a mistake. Then he spoke again. He started belting out, "He's gonna shoot! He's shooting! He's shooting!" I could still see movement, but no weapon yet. If they were shooting, I couldn't hear it in the commotion and I felt no rounds zinging past me either. But Krogh seemed *very* concerned that some *very* serious shit was coming down the pipe. I held my finger on the trigger, bracing for the worst.

Soon the left rear door of the Passat cracked open, shut, and then swung open fully. Immediately I thought of the TV shows like *Cops*, or really, any high-speed chase footage for that matter. At the end of the car chase the car either slows down or crashes, the door or doors swing open, and anywhere from one to four guys take off running in different directions. I assumed that was now happening. Like many Americans, I still believed that real life was much like TV.

Though the car was still traveling fast, I yelled, "They're gonna jump! They're gonna jump!" Suddenly, something came out of the open door. It was an *object*, but I couldn't tell what kind of . . .

The dive horn began blaring inside my head. Failure was suddenly not just an option. It was likely. For the first time in my life, someone was leveling an RPG at me, preparing to fire.

Mother. Fucker. TV had rotted my brain. The guys in the car had no intention of making a break for freedom. They wanted to scrap.

Why the RPG round did not fly off the launcher at that moment, slamming into the windshield of my humvee, killing all seven of us, I wouldn't find out until later that night. For the moment, though, I was using the extra microseconds to think. Suddenly the passenger—now officially a combatant—withdrew the RPG and the door swung shut—for a second. Then, to my surprise, it opened again.

We were now coming up quickly on a T-shaped intersection. As the car took a right turn, nearly flipping, the RPG was dropped out of the door, onto the road. We flew right past it. As we came around the corner behind the Passat, we were within fifteen feet of it. I could see people on the sidewalk scattering. It was as if they could sense the impending danger. The corner turned, I saw something else being raised in the back seat and pointed at me—either another RPG or an AK-47. This time I was not going to wait around to find out what it w—

Neither was Lawrence on the SAW. He squeezed the trigger on the machine gun and held it there. The sound of this weapon, not twelve inches from my head, was indescribable. It was *so fucking loud* that all I wanted was for it to be over. I wasn't just hearing it in my ears. It was penetrating into my head, making my brain tingle. I didn't know things could *be* that loud. Not to be outdone by Lawrence, and still aiming at the Volkswagen's back windshield, I started shooting . . . and shooting . . . and shooting. All I could think of was that we had no cover. If the gunmen packed inside the still-moving car were able to launch a single rocket-propelled grenade, we would be dead. The fear washed over me instantaneously with tsunami-like force. I suddenly became *desperate* to kill them before they got off a shot, and the only cover I could think of was to keep shooting. It wasn't a complete thought, though. I didn't have time for that. It was more like an instinct. I knew that a wall of lead was all we had.

My vision quickly became telescopic as the adrenaline forced me to focus on nothing but the back windshield of the car in front of us. All I could see was smoke, flying glass, and red tracers coming from my M4 and Lawrence's machine gun. Time and space no longer existed as it had only moments before. As I continued to fire into the back of the car, I felt like it would never end. At that moment, with death swirling around me, I felt like I couldn't be killed—like I was never going to die. Each time I pulled the trigger of the weapon I'd slept with for nearly two years, it felt like it had become an extension of my body—as if I were *willing* those in the Passat to die. And I couldn't pull the trigger fast enough.

Detachedly, I noticed Corn trying squirm between Lawrence and me. I could feel him trying to get in on the action. He managed to fire three or four rounds before he got squeezed out. Lawrence, on the other hand, continued to hammer away at the car by coldly and steadily using up his ammunition. The sounds and vibrations of our barrage began to swallow me up and my vision became tunneled. Because of that, I didn't see two gunmen roll out of the left door of the back seat. Lawrence did however, and he drew a bead on both of them, knocking them down with his second long burst from the SAW.

I kept firing into the back of the car. The cacophony of gunfire continued for an eternity—or five or ten seconds. Hot brass shell casings were pinging every which way—bouncing off the railings of the humvee, off of each other, onto the sand-bagged floor, onto the concrete below. Finally something in the trunk of this car, not twenty feet in front of us, made a popping noise and caught on fire.

The blue Volkswagen Passat rolled to a stop.

I'm in the bottom of a well. Someone is yelling, "Cease fire! Cease fire!" I know that I'm not shooting my gun anymore, but this is all I know.

I was still staring at the Volkswagen in the light of the streetlamps. I could feel people moving around me. *People are jumping out of the humvee. I'm not sure what to do. The barrel of my weapon is hot. It feels just like it does after we shoot at the range or in live fires. I have just finished firing it. I think I'm out of ammo. Is this real? Was I just in a shootout?*

Then I snapped back. *I should jump out of the humvee.* I moved.

The first thing I noticed was that we had clearly won the fight. There were bodies and shards of glass everywhere. There was blood starting to pool. The next thing I saw was a soldier from one of the other humvees open the front passenger door of the Passat and pull one of the men out. Apparently he was still alive. *Where did he come from . . . ?* Then I realized the other trucks had arrived without my noticing. The soldier threw him on the ground and kicked him in the face. Two other soldiers pounced on him and zip-tied his hands behind his back.

I turned around, looked back at the intersection, and started to move in that direction when I noticed the first RPG lying in the road. "Hey, I need some help over here," I called back in the direction of the Passat. No response. "Hey!" Nothing. Everyone was busy crawling all over the carnage. *Fuck it.* I ran out into the intersection and grabbed the RPG launcher. When I picked it up, the round started to fall out. Quickly, I moved to catch it before it hit the ground. *If it's been fired . . .* All I needed was for the round to detonate on contact. In the process of fumbling, I nearly dropped my weapon. Now I was juggling an M4, an RPG, and an RPG round. I couldn't fire my weapon. *Goddammit.* I hurried awkwardly back to scene of the action with my armload of weaponry and carefully deposited the launcher and round on the sidewalk next to . . .

Suddenly I saw what had been pulled from the car. Lying on the sidewalk beside the Passat were two RPG launchers, three RPG rounds, two AK-47s, seven magazines, and four hand grenades. All three RPG rounds were armed and the one I had picked up had been fired. Its fuse had been ignited, but for some reason it hadn't gone off.

I'm back in the Shah-e-Kot Valley, where Takhur Gar looms above me. I've just been told that the thing that fell out of the sky on my platoon's position mere moments ago was a two-thousand-pound satellite guided bomb dropped by an air force F-16. No one knows yet why it didn't go off. It would have killed all of us. I would never get a satisfactory explanation.

Now, nineteen months later, it's happened again. As of that moment, I should have been dead twice. Not in the "that sure was close" way you experience in busy interstate traffic, but in the "This is no shit—I'm really not supposed to be here anymore" way.

Stepping off the sidewalk, I looked around. I noticed that the driver was still in the front seat, slumped over the steering wheel. I walked over to the two men who had rolled out of the still moving car. They were alive.

The first one out of the car, the RPG gunner, was sitting cross-legged in the street behind the Passat. He was wearing khakis and a white button-down, short sleeve shirt, and he was pudgy. Hands zip-tied behind his back, he had taken two rounds in the gut. He was bleeding, but I'd seen worse. For having been shot through the abdomen twice, he seemed in relatively good shape. As for his health in general, the picture wasn't as rosy. He was drenched in sweat and his breathing was labored. I could see his chest heaving up and down. Waseem was standing there with me. I turned to him and said, "Waseem, ask this dude, 'What the fuck?' Ask him why they did this." Waseem leaned down and said something in Arabic. Through labored breathing, Mr. RPG said something softly to Waseem. Waseem stood back up.

"What'd he say?" I asked.

"He says 'Take us to the hospital.' "

I shook my head and looked down at the guy. He looked up, his eyes meeting mine for the first time. "Go fuck yourself," I said.

Waseem and I walked over to the RPG guy's backseat friend. He was lying face down in the gutter on the side of the street. He had been shot through the knee, and it already looked like a purple and black cantaloupe. His leg was twisted behind him at a somewhat disturbing angle. Sergeant Collins was standing over him trying to direct some of the guys to place this guy in the back of one of the humvees. As soon as the first soldier touched the guy's leg he let out a blood-curdling cry. It was like nothing I've ever heard before. Instead of a scream, it was more reminiscent of an animal-like howl. It sent a shiver down my spine.

"Waseem," Sergeant Collins said impatiently, "tell this guy we're tryin' to help him."

Waseem leaned down and translated the message. When they picked the wounded man up the second time and set him in the bed of the humvee, he only let out a few involuntary squeaks and grunts.

I walked to the Passat where some of the guys were extracting the driver. His brains were all over the dash and the windshield. He had been shot in the head twice. One round had exited out of his left eye. In all, we hit the driver with maybe ten rounds. I figured a few of them were mine. There was blood everywhere. I thought to myself that this guy had really taken the brunt of it. Someone brought up later that if the RPG *had* gone off, the backblast would have killed him anyway. Just wasn't his night, I guess.

I looked at Collins and thought I could feel what he was thinking as he surveyed the scene of crumpled bodies before him. He must have been satisfied—after two years, our platoon—*his platoon*—had finally achieved a state of carnage.

Around the other side of the car, the guman who had been beaten was still lying face down in the street. He had closely cropped hair and was wearing black parachute pants. He had been wearing a white tank top, but the guys had since torn it to ribbons during the scuffle after they pulled him from the car. I could see several marks on the guy, including a nasty cut across the bridge of his nose where he'd been kicked. The only bullet wound was on the left side of his head. It was only a grazing wound, but heads bleed profusely, and he was covered in blood.

Yet something about his wounds didn't seem right. I walked back over to the Passat and looked into the front passenger seat. It was peppered, *riddled*, with bullet holes. I looked back at the guy lying face down on the ground, and then back into the car. The holes were still there, lots and lots of them. Stuffing was showing in places. I looked back at the guy. One partial hole in his head. I looked into the car again. *What the fuck?* For a moment I thought that we had hit one of the running civilians, but then I remembered this guy being pulled from the car. I showed some other guys and they just shrugged. I couldn't imagine how he'd managed to sustain one grazing bullet wound under such an intense hail of gunfire. I didn't know why he was basically untouched when his seat had been shot to shreds. But I did know that I should have been dead at least twice, and yet here I was, still hanging on. These things happen, I guess. You just accept them, move on, and don't tell your mother.

The expression "dead weight" comes from dead people. I'd never thought about that until I got to Iraq, until we had to get the wasted driver in the back of a humvee. The operation was more complicated than it sounds. Not only heavy, the guy was also a mess. He was bloody and nasty and no one wanted to touch him, much less wrap their arms around him.

Sergeant Collins had the idea that four guys should grab one appendage each. One guy on each arm and leg. In unison, the idea went, they would swing him, and on the count of three, they would launch him into the bed of the truck. He thought that would be the most hygienic way to handle it.

This was a good plan, and it worked on the second try. When they threw him on the first attempt, someone's timing was off and the lifeless guy's head hit the side of the humvee. It made a sickening *"thok"* sound that made me want to puke. The sound must have startled the guys too, because as soon as his head hit the truck, they dropped him. His arms and legs were splayed everywhere and when his head hit the asphalt, it made an even more revolting *"thok"* than when it had hit the humvee. Guys groaned at the gruesome sight. After a few seconds and a few deep breaths, they tried again, this time successfully.

As we rolled slowly away from the scene, I could see a throng of Iraqis gathered on the sidewalks up ahead. The city hadn't seen this level of violence in a long time, and word traveled fast in Tal Afar.

As we drove, no one said anything. The silence in my truck mirrored the stillness of the crowd. They all knew what had happened. As we continued slowly through the mass of citizenry, it looked like a macabre, twisted sort of Mardi Gras parade.

When we arrived back at the TOC, all of Bravo Company and the entire Battalion headquarters section were outside waiting. The medics had already set up an emergency casualty treatment area outside in the courtyard. When we first arrived back, I was disoriented. Everyone who had been back at the TOC listening to the play-by-play on the radio was grinning from ear to ear. The air at the TOC was electric. As soon as we dismounted, everyone at the TOC mobbed us. It was like a media crush.

I didn't get it at first. All I wanted to do was to sit down and have some time for personal reflection. But everybody there wanted to know *exactly* what happened. Like little kids waiting for Christmas presents. To them, the shooting meant vindication for the deaths of Jordan and Garvey. We had been hurt on that night, and now someone, whether or not they had anything to do with that attack, had paid. On that night, as a battalion, we not only lost two friends and soldiers, but the attackers had taken our pride and shaken our confidence. But now, the enemy was no longer elusive and invisible. He wasn't the boogeyman. He was flesh and blood. Lots and lots of it.

The medics were working furiously to save the lives of the wounded attackers in true American fashion. At the same time, Hameed was interrogating them in true Iraqi fashion. As our physician's assistant toiled away, attempting to keep Mr. RPG's intestines from falling out of his body, Hameed stood over him getting irate. His eyes were like hot coals and I could see spittle coming out of the sides of his mouth as he spoke to the man. He was seething with anger, ready to push the Doc out of the way and throttle the guy right there on the stretcher. When he was finished, he walked over in my direction.

"Hey Hameed, what'd you say to that guy?" I asked curiously.

"I tell him," he said in heavily accented English, "I make

him eat his own guts if he doesn't give us information."

"Oooookay," I replied, not quite sure how to respond to a statement like that. *Sounds good Hameed, keep up the good work.* "So, did he say anything?" I asked.

"Yah, he says he was paid twenty-five dollars to attack TOC."

I rolled my eyes and shook my head.

After a while, I walked back to the barracks building. Several guys had started photographing themselves with the dead body and I wasn't interested. I was neither interested in participating, nor in putting a stop to it. I just didn't care anymore. They could have started playing soccer with his head and it wouldn't have made a difference to me.

Detachedly, I wondered what was happening to us. I thought about how I had once gotten angry with the sergeant for shoving the kid in Baghdad. I thought about how bad I felt after the bags went on the heads of the looters on our first full day in that city. Back then I had cared. I looked at my watch. It was 11:57 p.m. on a night in October. After only seven months in Iraq we were becoming savages. I wasn't sure whether that was a good thing or a bad thing.

I couldn't sit down either. I was too wired. I walked back over to the TOC, where most of the guys in 1st Platoon were at the computers, emailing the news to family and friends back home. I asked if we could use the satellite phone. Seconds later it was in my hand.

I called my dad on his cell phone.

"Hello?"

"Hey, how's it goin'," I asked.

There was a pause. "Great!" he said as soon as he recognized my voice. "This is a surprise. I didn't expect to hear from you for a while. What are you doin'? What time is it there?"

"Yeah," I said, "it's almost midnight here." I paused. "Well, first, how's Grandpa?" The old marine was in the hospital and the doctors didn't think the prognosis was very promising.

"He's hanging in there," my dad said, "but your mother is still pretty upset all the time."

"Yeah . . . ," I paused. "So what are you doing right now?" I asked.

"Oh, I'm at the gas station getting the oil changed."

Real life, I thought. *It's daytime there and he's getting his oil changed. People are being normal and going about their daily lives.*

"I'm glad you called," he said. "We hadn't heard from you in a while. So what are you doing up at midnight calling me?"

"Well," I said, "the strangest thing just happened . . . ."

So I told him the story. Then I walked back to the barracks. Nobody in 1st Platoon could sleep. We stayed up most of the night talking—going over and over every detail of what had happened. At three o'clock in the morning, I finally grabbed a cot. Lying there, I remembered a line I'd read in a book about Vietnam. It was called *Everything We Had* and it was a collection of stories told by veterans and compiled by Al Santoli. An infantry officer who had also been in the 101st had remarked at the end of his story, "What a fucking way to live your life."

As I drifted off to sleep, two hours before the sunrise, that's all I could think of. *What a fucking way to live your life.*

Eventually I made it to the airfield. I spent my last few days there eating at Kellogg, Brown, and Root's fancy new chow hall and emailing people, mostly my mom. She was updating me on my grandfather's condition, while at the same time grilling me on how safe my convoy to Mosul would be. Though the whole war thing had never sat well with her, she was beginning to panic because the insurgency had begun to snowball all across northern Iraq in the last week.

Two days before I left, I met Croom and some of the guys for lunch at the chow hall. It had been several days since the shooting and I hadn't yet seen anyone from 3rd Platoon. "What the fuck happened, man? You're not supposed to be gettin' in shootouts anymore. You're on the way out, for chrissake," were the first words out of Croom's mouth. He grinned and then sank his teeth into a corncob, waiting for me to tell him the story.

So I gave him the rundown. But since I'd spent the first half of the deployment telling him stories about Anaconda, it seemed strange to be telling him about my experiences in Iraq—as if I were telling some random soldier, and not the guy with whom I'd been closest for the first half of our time in Iraq. Somehow, my most intense combat experiences had straddled the time in which we'd worked together.

I told him how tunnel-visioned I'd gotten, and how I hadn't been able to see anything but the car once the shooting started. I also told him that I hadn't been trying to save the guys' lives around me, or trying to prevent an imminent attack on the TOC. Instead, I told him that I'd been trying to make my way down to the airfield for a good night's rest and ended up fighting to save my own life. Not very noble, I said, but fuck it. That's combat in a guerilla war for you.

* * *

I spent the rest of the week hounding Shields about the issue of weapons on the bus ride from Tal Afar to the Mosul airfield. If you were one of these soldiers, you weren't allowed to carry a weapon because you were leaving the country—and brigade wouldn't assign anybody to handle the return of all the weapons to Tal Afar. All they did was provide a heavy weapons platoon escort, along with armed guards on the bus. The trip hadn't been a problem for most of the summer, but now, with the violence escalating, I considered it a major one. I was convinced that the person who devised the rule was a person who rarely traveled the roads of northern Iraq.

Shields and the battalion mail clerk, Damian Heidelberg, were going to be the armed guards on our bus as we drove to Mosul. For that reason I pestered Shields all week to see if he could find a way to allow me to hold on to my weapon. After having an RPG pulled on me several days earlier, the idea of riding through western Mosul's ambush alley unarmed seemed insane to me. Even the idea of getting up off my cot to go take a shit without my weapon had grown disturbing in the past few days. I didn't care if there was a gun truck escort or not. I wanted a gun and I wanted bullets.

In the end, I grudgingly boarded the bus without a weapon, taking a seat behind Heidelberg. I looked over his shoulder and gazed longingly at the M4 sitting in his lap. It was the weapon of a mail clerk—no special sight, no infrared laser on top, no tactical flashlight mounted on the side of the barrel. Just a gun with a plain, old-fashioned iron sight.

Before I knew who Heidelberg was, he'd approached me out of the blue one day while I was picking up Delta

Company's mail with Sergeant Croom.

"Hey, Lieutenant Friedman, here's a letter for you. I just found it. It was in the Bravo Company stack."

I don't know this guy's name, but he continues walking toward me. "I just saw it lying there and told the guy that put it there that you hadn't been in Bravo Company for months."

I look at him curiously and take it from him, glancing down at the return address. I see that it's from my parents. I look back up at this person who obviously knows who I am and can only assume that he is our battalion mail clerk.

Heidelberg fit the mail clerk stereotype. He knew the name of every soldier in the battalion, what his rank was, and what company he was in. He took his job seriously, too, braving the Tal Afar-to-Mosul run every few days to gather our mail and other needed supplies. Heidelberg spent most of his time knee-deep in letters and packages, trying desperately to find some way in which to organize them all.

Now sitting on the freedom bus, with the mail clerk as my security, I tapped him on the shoulder. "Must be nice . . . getting to carry a weapon."

He turned around. "Oh, hey, sir. I didn't see you there. What? Oh, nah, what am I gonna do with this thing anyway? You know?"

"I'd take a pair of brass knuckles if I could get them right now," I said.

He looked away as if he were thinking of something. "Hey sir, you were in that firefight the other night, weren't you?"

I nodded.

He paused again. "Why don't you take my weapon, sir? You'd be better with it than me anyway. You're an infantryman."

My instinct was to say no, but I stopped short. For a split second I thought about it. He was right, but I didn't know if he *really* wanted to give his weapon away knowing the risks. I didn't know if he was just trying to be nice or if I was passively applying pressure from a higher rank. I looked him in the eye and asked, "You sure?"

"Yeah," he said. "You could use it more than me."

He handed me the M4 as the bus approached the airfield gate. In a way, he had just put his life in my hands. I wanted to believe that I was a better shot than Heidelberg, and that he knew it. I wanted to think that we had done the math and both knew we'd be better off if I took the gun. In reality, I think I just wanted something to hold onto. I took one look at the other people on the bus and then tapped the magazine in the well. I charged the handle, chambering a round.

Being extracted—whether it's from one battlefield or an entire war zone— is when you start to believe that you've made it through. You get euphoric, but in the back of your mind you realize there's still time to get killed. You're about to get out of class for summer, but you haven't gotten that last report card yet. It's the time in which you promise yourself that, *I will never do anything like this ever again.* Even though somewhere deep inside, you know you're lying to yourself.

Dusk is rapidly becoming night on our last night in the Shah-e-Kot Valley. I'm standing in a draw, watching my own breath. A neck gaiter clings snugly around my neck, while my helmet and night vision still lie on the hard, frozen ground. I look up and see the night's first few stars beginning to appear.

From behind a rock wall, our chaplain comes walking down a path with his security assistant. It's the first time I realize that chaplains don't carry guns. They've come from the high ground and Charlie Company.

I spend a few minutes talking to him about how some units have already been pulled from the valley, and how our security is slightly more compromised tonight than on any other night. I tell him the steps we've taken to make sure that nothing will happen to will prevent our getting out of here safely in the morning.

Less troops meaning less security is something that hasn't occurred to the chaplain yet. Not having intended to startle him, I tell him it's no big deal and not to worry about it.

That's when we see a strange light appear on a ridge across the valley. He asks me what it could be, and I tell him I have no idea. It's so far away that I figure it doesn't concern us. For all I know, it could be Osama bin Laden.

But the chaplain is concerned. "Hey man, do you think it's safe for me to make my way down to you guys' CP?"

"Yeah," I say. "As long as you stay on this path all the way there, somebody from Bravo Company—whether you see him or not—has got his eyes on you." His face tells me that he's not convinced. He glances up again at the mysterious light in the distance.

"I think that light's moved. Are you sure you think it's safe?"

"Yeah, you'll be okay," I try to reassure him. "That light's probably a friendly unit."

As the two of them amble down the trail, I hope they'll be okay. We're too close to being out of here.

When I awake the next morning, the first thing I hear on the radio is that our extraction has been delayed by twenty-four hours. This is a kick in the balls.

But nothing happens that day. Even the al Qaeda anti-aircraft gun on the mountain has been silenced through bombing. That evening, just as the clear blue sky is beginning to turn purple, Sergeant Collins and I find ourselves staring at the Whale on the far side of the valley. We see tiny troops on horseback silhouetted against the skyline on top of the ridge. For me at least, it's a wonderful sight—Zia's troops have returned after over a week in hiding. I'm not so sure if Collins is happy, however. He's spent all this time in the valley being cold, and hasn't gotten to see a single drop of anyone's lifeblood run out.

Early the next afternoon I get the radio call that the birds are on the way. First comes the whine of the Apache escorts, followed by the familiar thumping of a Chinook's twin rotor blades. The Chinook tries to land but throws up too much dust, causing the pilot to abort. For an instant my heart sinks as I realize I may have to spend another night out here in the valley. But then he returns, this time touching down safely.

After I'm safely hooked into the aircraft, I think to myself, I will never do anything like this ever again.

Halfway between Tal Afar and Mosul, I started thinking again about the horse from the valley. In my haste to leave the Shah-e-Kot forever I had forgotten to check to see if the maddened animal was still alive. Looking out over the hills of northern Iraq, the sun just beginning to rise in front of us, I hoped the horse had made it out too. I sat there wanting to believe that he was still out there, and that a returned owner was caring for him. I hoped he was filling himself up with green grass on a peaceful valley floor, and that he'd forgotten about everything that happened.

The ride couldn't have gone smoother. We cruised through ambush alley without a hitch, arriving at the Mosul airfield in less than forty-five minutes. When we offloaded the bus, I found Heidelberg standing beside the bags. I walked over to him and handed him back his weapon.

I said, "Thanks, man. You know you didn't have to do that."

"Oh it was no problem, sir," he said with a smile.

I was still confounded by the idea that he had voluntarily relinquished his weapon in a situation like that. I said, "Well all right. Take care then. Keep all that mail straight."

He came back with, "I will, sir. See you back at Fort Campbell."

Shortly after I left, the intensity of the insurgency around Tal Afar ramped up. A week later somebody threw a grenade at 2nd Platoon. A while after that, 3rd Platoon was ambushed not far from where we'd shot up the Passat. It was bloody. An RPG took off a squad leader's leg at the hip. Civilians were caught in the crossfire. Children died. On another night, a suicide bomber tried to drive into the TOC. He almost made it before being shot to pieces and detonating his cargo. It wounded nearly sixty guys in Bravo. Roadside bombs started going off like black cats on a string. Shootings became commonplace.

But when Damian Heidelberg was shot down in a Black Hawk helicopter a month after I left, I took it the hardest. It made me hate myself. Not because I'd known him personally, but because as his body fell to the earth in a spinning, burning wreck, I was home safe and sound, out of danger and sleeping beneath the covers of a warm bed.

Part III

RECOVERY

Yes, these are bruises from fighting.
Yes, I'm comfortable with that. I am
enlightened.

—Narrator, *Fight Club*

10

Amrika

Fall 2003

Mike Bandzwolek, my 1st Platoon successor, was on leave at Fort Campbell the cool October night that I flew in, so I had him pick me up at the battalion headquarters. Mike had talked to my parents over the phone and said they were waiting for me at their hotel. They still hadn't forgiven themselves for not being there when I got off the plane from Afghanistan, so they'd made it a point to be in Clarksville this time.

I was feeling numb and thought about asking Mike if he wanted to get some beer after I spent some time with my parents. I knew I wouldn't sleep that night for a couple of reasons. One, I was jet-lagged, and two, I'd gotten drunk off of two Guinnesses at the airport bar in Shannon, Ireland, and had passed out somewhere over the Atlantic.

They were standing outside the hotel when we got there—the way two expectant parents might wait for a four-year-old after his first full day of school. Mike found a parking space and I jumped out. But rather than run to my parents, I walked to the bed of his truck and started unloading my bags. A second later, I realized what I was doing and turned just as my mom reached me. She put her arms around me and started squeezing. When she finally let me go, I saw my dad standing there. I wasn't sure whether we were going to hug or just shake hands. It was awkward for some reason, but I wasn't sure why. He put his arms around me in a giant bear hug.

Mike saw what was going on and decided to throw off the rest of my bags before getting back in his truck to leave. I told him I'd call him. As I watched his red tail lights head toward Wilma Rudolph Boulevard, I asked my mom how my grandfather was. She said not so well.

All of a sudden I started in on her. "What are you doing here? Why aren't you in Shreveport with him? I told you to stay home with him if he was in bad shape. I told you I'd be fine here." I could hear myself, and I sounded irritated. Not like someone who'd just seen his parents for the first time in nearly a year.

She looked taken aback, maybe even hurt. I'm sure it had been an agonizing decision for her, whether or not to leave her father's cancer-stricken side, and now I was criticizing her for making the wrong one.

I apologized on the way to my apartment. We hung out for a while making small talk before they got tired and decided to head back to the hotel. Where there had been no invisible barrier between us before the deployment, now, I could tell, there was. We could touch hands and smile through the clear glass pane, but there was no warmth, no human touch. I could hear their words but they came flat to my ears—like I was listening through earplugs. Everything was flat—the few things I divulged about the war, the way I expressed myself. I felt like I had to hold up the carcass of a dead personality and make it move and talk so that I could show my parents that it was still animate.

After they left I couldn't sleep. I decided to walk to the Super Wal-Mart just down the street, the only place still open at half past two in the morning. Shortly after stepping inside, I knew I had a problem. There were people there I didn't know, I didn't have a weapon, and there were no soldiers around me. I got what I needed and left as quickly as I could.

The next morning I got up early, threw some clothes in a bag, and walked over to the hotel at which my parents were staying. When I walked in the room, my mom was sitting on the bed with her back to me. She turned around when she heard me approach and stood up to face me. Then she broke down crying. I looked at my dad, not sure what was happening.

He said, "We lost Grandpa last night."

I looked at my mom and said, "Oh. I'm sorry." I felt like it should have affected me in some way, but there wasn't really anything there.

We went to the funeral in Shreveport two days later. Everyone was upset and crying. But to me it didn't seem like a big deal. He was a marine. He'd made it through his war and lived a successful life. He had three kids, five grandkids, and had lived a happy retirement, traveling the world with my grandmother. I couldn't make myself sad even when I consciously tried to. In my warped mind, I felt that I'd just come from a place where soldiers and Marines were being robbed of their chances to have kids, grandkids, and happy retirements spent traveling with their wives. The way I saw it, he'd done pretty well. To me, there was nothing to cry about.

I was in such a daze that I might have even said this to someone in my family. I can't remember.

For six weeks back at Fort Campbell I went to work in the morning, came home in the afternoon, and started drinking around early evening. It was during that period that 3rd Platoon got ambushed. Then one morning after a run, Nick Bilotta, the Charlie Company guy who'd been wounded that day in Baghdad, told me that Heidelberg was KIA. Several weeks after that, the car bomb exploded at the TOC. I sat there on my bed, beer in hand, watching the report about the car bomb on the news. They even interviewed the guy who had replaced me as XO. I sat there wondering just what in the fuck I was doing in Clarksville, Tennessee, while all this was going on in my company.

Finally, on a blustery but sunny December day on Fort Campbell, I signed out of the Army. I had no job lined up, graduate school didn't start for another eight months, and Nikki was in Dallas with an architect. I had nowhere else to go, so I went home.

In 2002 I spent nine months in the United States between the wars in Afghanistan and Iraq. Besides the growing gap between Nikki and me, this is what I remember about that period . . . .

Sergeant Collins is sponsoring another keg party on the deck at his house. I'm there fraternizing, though, as far as I'm concerned, the idea is laughable after you've gone to war together. By nine o'clock the keg is floated and we're completely wasted.

By ten o'clock the party has moved to the Lighthouse down on Riverside Drive. By eleven I'm standing in a corner of the club with Kamauf and Smerbeck, no women for miles. The three of us are slurring to each other about how important going to Afghanistan was. And how at the time, we didn't think Anaconda was such a big deal, but that it really was a big deal. How it was the real shit.

By midnight, Kamauf and I have been tossed out of the bar. Everything is spinning and I can't remember why we got bounced. Maybe a fight, maybe too drunk. Neither of us drove so we decide to hump it back to Jimbo's house to sleep. It's four miles away, but our infantry egos and the alcohol tell us that that's not such a big deal.

A mile down the road I'm peeling Kamauf up off the concrete. I stumble in the process and we end up helping each other back to our feet, laughing like idiots. Kamauf suggests we get off the sidewalk and move along the river side of the barrier so that we don't attract any cops. I agree.

His good intentions don't take into account that the barrier is there in the first place to prevent cars from taking the curve too fast and hurtling into the river. By one o'clock he is trying to pull me out of the brambles on the side of the hill. He goes down with me, and together we slip farther toward the river. Red Bull and vodka has intensified the earth's gravitational pull to the extent that this slight incline overlooking the river might as well be a sheer rock face. I come close to gaining a foothold and then tumble farther down. I can hear the water. I can hear my own laughter. In the faint streetlight coming from the top of the hill I can see that the branches and thorns in the brush have cut my hands.

We claw our way back up to the top, away from the river. Back on the sidewalk, we can't stop laughing at each other. My khakis have been torn to ribbons; my right leg is bleeding through what's left of them. In a marble-mouthed haze, Kamauf asks me if I have my cell phone on me. He says we should call somebody. I manage to say yes, unless I lost it, unable to recall why I hadn't thought about that sooner.

It is time to radio the QRF.

I thought maybe the homecoming would go smoother the second time around. I made it a point to see Nikki when she was in town around Christmas. It was nearly a year to the day since I'd walked out of her apartment. We talked briefly over lunch at a restaurant. She said she was happy. After that I never spoke to her again.

I never drank around my family during the day, but the short temper and the mood swings did enough damage. One night after I couldn't find something of mine that my poor mom had unwittingly moved, I blew my top. When I calmed down fifteen minutes later, I realized just how stupid I looked and sounded. It made me laugh. I was becoming a stereotype. Johnny had come marching home just like the rest of the infantry.

Hanging out at home with Mom and Dad, trying to function just after the war, I could tell, just wasn't going to work out. It was after I yelled at my parents for touching my shit that I decided to leave. I'd had enough of my family, my hometown, all the superficial news stories about the war, and the plethora of "support the troops" stickers on cars. I was tired of everyone's shallow patriotism. Everyone around me had an opinion about what we should do to "the Iraqis" and the "terrorists," but nine out of ten of them couldn't tell the difference between the two. I was surrounded by supporters of the government—often those closest to me—who had no knowledge of history or insurgencies; no sense of real patriotism. In my mind, flags and stickers did not count as patriotism. To them it was a fight to defend freedom and that was all there was to it. We *love* freedom; they *hate* freedom. We must defend *liberty*. From the safety of their cozy bedrooms, watching other people deal with REAL PROBLEMS on the TV from ten thousand miles away, that was the attitude. There was no depth of reflection, no critical thinking. There was no respect for the true nature of a bloody life-and-death clash of human cultures and ideologies. There was no empathy for Iraqi families. Roger Waters of Pink Floyd called this kind of mentality "the bravery of being out of range," and he wrote a song about it.

I just felt like I didn't belong there anymore. America had somehow become *Amrika*, as the Iraqis say. I was on the outside looking in, and I needed space.

So I took the money and ran—using the cash I'd saved during the two wars. In army-speak I "beat feet." I "popped smoke." Less than ninety days after setting foot back on American soil, I caught a military hop headed for Europe. I figured that would be far enough away. All I carried was a single backpack with clothes, some photographs, a camera, and my passport. There were no plans for returning home. The first lesson I'd learned on returning from a guerilla war was this: Get your fucking head on straight before you speak to anyone.

11

The Mediterranean

Winter 2004

On the Spanish island of Mallorca, an explosion tore through the cold night air. We had been drinking up on the roof of the place I'd been staying. I was with two other lone travelers. One was American and the other a French Canadian. Sitting in lawn chairs that overlooked Palma harbor, we had been staring at all the twinkling lights on the hundreds of yachts down below. For three days I had told neither of them that I'd been in the American army.

It was earsplitting and close. I was out of my chair and moving for cover before the echo had stopped reverberating. As I moved in a low crouch, I turned and looked back at the two guys. They hadn't moved and looked like seated statues. The Canadian had a Heineken halfway to his lips, where it was now paused. They were staring at me.

"Wow, man. You okay?" he asked. His French accent sounded to me vaguely like Ammar's Arabic one.

A car backfire, magnified by crisp, clear night air and tall buildings set closely together, does not necessarily register as "car backfire" to skittish ears. As I thought about how to explain my reaction, I realized that I didn't even jump like that when I was in theater. Two wars, and I don't think I ever jumped like that. I guessed that it had something to do with not being around any other soldiers, being halfway buzzed, and not clutching a weapon.

I spent the rest of the night killing a twelve-pack under the stars, telling war stories.

Over sangria in Barcelona I told a psychology grad student what the moment is like right before you die. When I did that, I felt like I was using my real voice for the first time in a while. It felt *fresh*. When I spoke of the war, it didn't have that flat tone anymore.

When she finally asked me how I was doing, I paused, trying to figure out how to answer her. I'd gotten the same question from a lot of people back home. Usually they would start by asking me what the war was like. Then they'd ask how it affected me. And then, as if to make themselves more comfortable, they'd always say with a laugh, "But you're okay now, right?"

Every time I'd hear something like that, I'd hear Ving Rhames' character in *Pulp Fiction* when Bruce Willis asks him if *he's* okay. This, of course, is after the disconcerting rape scene with the red ball gags and the gimp. Rhames' character, Marsellus Wallace, responds, "Naw, man. I'm pretty fuckin' far from okay."

To Lisa, the curious junior psychoanalyst I'd known for three days, I responded, "I'll be fine."

In a train car, on the way to Rome, I stayed awake all night talking war and international affairs with an Australian accountant. I'd been traveling with him and an American girl for two weeks and he hadn't really probed about the war or what I thought about it.

As the train clacked along the tracks, we played cards, and I told him about how, in the beginning, a reasoning, moral person could have wanted to do the things I'd done, and see the things I'd seen. Crossing the Italian frontier, I told him about the Iraqi people I'd met like Ammar, Mohamed, and Waseem. I tried to convey to him how awkward it was at times for the Iraqis to work with the Americans. And I recounted how Hameed had threatened to make the RPG gunner eat his own guts. After that I glanced over at the sleeping girl next to us. She looked peaceful. I dealt the stack of cards and continued on. I tried to explain to him Collins' seemingly unquenchable lust for battle—and how even that had seemed to wane, or *soften*, toward the end. I told him about Croom and what a great guy he was. And I explained to him how Croom had once told me he'd lost his faith in God on 9/11. A few hands later I turned the deck over and said, "Your turn to shuffle, dude."

In Rome I met a sergeant with a group of American soldiers who were partying away their leave from the American base at Vicenza. Their closely cropped hair had given them away. Over the din of a noisy bar, we talked about Iraq. He'd been in Kirkuk around the same time I was there, and we talked about how shitty things were getting in northern Iraq. We tried to come up with some names of people we knew in common, but couldn't think of any.

Talking to him, I'd never felt more awkward—there with my longish hair, backpacking around a continent with no responsibility—talking to those who were preparing to go back to war. I felt out of place again, like some hirsute hippie.

I wanted to feel *in* place again, to be comfortable somewhere. I think that's why a part of me was trying to get back to the Middle East—to the Arab world—to the only place I really knew how to *be*. I knew how things worked there and I knew where I stood there.

I took another train to the Italian port of Brindisi, this time alone. I was being pulled southeast by what was becoming a sort of tractor beam. Along the route through the Campanian countryside I talked to no one. I just let my mind drift. I thought back on how I'd done. I was twenty-five years old and I'd been a combatant in two wars already. I thought about how, as a kid, it was something I'd always envisioned—wanted, needed. But somehow it hadn't turned out the way I thought it would. I never thought that battle was something that could drive a spike into my psyche the way it had.

I always thought it would have been easier. The soul-crushing phenomenon of fear before combat had been unexpected. It had left me more afraid of dying than ever. The idea terrifies me now. It keeps me awake at night. Before the wars, the thought of not being alive had warranted no more than a detached shrug. Now I could see that it would always be in the forefront of my mind—that it would be evident in everything I did. The closeness—that *proximity*—to death, or just the possibility of it, day in and day out seemed to have invaded my soul like a creeping disease. As the train clipped through southern Italy, I stared out the window.

From Brindisi I took an eight-hour ferry ride to Greece. Halfway across the Adriatic, I started dozing. There were

Greeks sitting, lounging, and talking around me. I allowed their language to put me to sleep. They were discussing something funny because they kept laughing while I lay there with my eyes closed and my book on my chest. After a while, though, it seemed like their conversation turned serious. It was a slight change in voice tone that I noticed. They began speaking *in Arabic*:

The Baghdad taxi driver won't stop yammering at me. I see he wants help for the people in his car. He is quivering anxiously, pacing and pointing for me to inspect his cargo. I see that the trunk of his taxi is half open. I walk over to it and look inside. The first thing I notice is all the blood. Looking up at me is an Iraqi man wearing shorts and a t-shirt. His eyes are as big as plates and he looks terrified. He has been shot but I can't tell how many times. His face is pale and his teeth are chattering. He is lying in a pool of his own blood.

"What about the other guy?" I say, gently setting the trunk lid back down. "Let's see the other guy."

Croom walks over and grabs the rear door handle. He opens it and looks in.

"Ohhh shit!" he says, taking a step back.

I walk around from the trunk and look inside. Blood, pink flesh, chips of bone, matted hair, lolling, vacant eyes, the muffled groan of—

I jerked and woke up, looking around and trying to get my bearings. The Greeks were still talking and hadn't seemed to notice. If they did, they hadn't cared.

I reached down to the ground and picked up my book where it had fallen. I put it back in my bag and then stood up. I stretched my back and walked out onto the deck of the ship. The wind was blowing and it was cool out. I stood with my hands on the railing, listening to the water lapping against the side of the ship. Across the water to the east was the Albanian coastline, with its soaring, snow-dusted mountains. As the setting sun reflected off the snow, it reminded me of the Hindu Kush. They looked just like the massive peaks ringing the Shomali plain in Afghanistan.

I stood there gazing out at them, wondering if I was always going to think that way. A part of me hoped that maybe one day they would just be mountains again.

There is an old trick that shady Athenians play on tourists. I'd read about it in a tourist book in Rome. It goes something like this: A native strikes up a friendly conversation with a lone tourist. After the tourist becomes comfortable with the Athenian, the Greek says he knows a great bar nearby with cheap drinks. He says there will probably be girls there and then he offers to take the tourist. Unbeknownst to the tourist, everyone in the bar is typically in on the ruse. The Greek buys the first round and gets the conversation going. Suddenly two beautiful women appear and begin conversing with the tourist. They start pouring it on—to the point that the tourist thinks he might have a chance with one or both of them. The tourist starts buying more drinks, becoming more inebriated with each one. Once he's ready to leave, the bartender hands him the check. The tourist sees three of them at this point, but he looks at the amount on the one in the middle. It's exorbitant—several hundred euros. The tourist at first argues. When he gets nowhere, he turns to the door. Only now, three very large men are blocking his way out. The bartender wants his money. The tourist looks for the guy who brought him there in the first place, but suddenly, the guy is nowhere to be seen.

I counted myself as being one of the fortunate ones for having heard of the scam before first wandering the maze of Athenian streets. Because I was on the lookout for it, I didn't let the prospect stop me from talking to the people I met.

One cloudy afternoon I was walking along a downtown street when a guy in drag walked past me going the other way. I did a double take just to make sure. A plump older gentleman wearing a dark coat and a Burberry scarf was walking just behind me and saw the same thing. After he/she had passed, I made eye contact with the older man and he said something to me in Greek—a joke by the expression on his face. I smiled politely and said, "Sorry, I don't speak Greek."

His eyes brightened. "Oh," he said, "you speak English. You American?" As he spoke, I noticed his wavy salt and pepper hair was just beginning to bald in the back.

I said, "Yes."

"Oh, that's great," he continued with a Greek accent. "My son lives in San Antonio. What part of the States you from?"

I told him I was from Louisiana but that I was moving to Texas when I got home. We walked and talked for a while during which time he told me his son was a doctor. He was dressed nicer than anyone around and I thought that might have explained it. He asked me if I'd eaten and I said no. "In that case," he said, "there's a sidewalk café just down the block. You wanna get a bite to eat?"

I was hungry so I said okay.

The downtown streets were packed, leaving us to thread our way through the moving crowd. He stopped for a moment outside a door to a building. The sign was in Greek. The rotund man looked up at me and said, "I'm going to run in here and grab a drink before we go. You can wait right here." Then he paused, appearing to think about it. "Or," he said, "you can come in and grab one too. It'll just take a second."

I wasn't sure what kind of a drink he meant, whether he wanted bottled water, a Gatorade, or a shot of ouzo, but I didn't object.

He opened the door, revealing a flight of stairs leading down. I followed him and when we reached the door at the bottom, he opened it and allowed me to proceed in first. Starting to feel a small prickle of uncertainty, I scanned the interior. As I did, I heard the man close the door behind me.

Mother. Fucker. To my right was the bar. Behind it stood a smiling, fiftyish looking female bartender. Sitting at the bar was the twentyish looking blond decoy—also smiling intently at me. I probably should have run right then, pushing through the man, and making my way back up the stairs, but I didn't. I figured that I'd play it cool and see if I could play stupid enough to get my wallet and myself out of this in one piece.

The fat man walked me over to the bar. "You want some ouzo," he asked. "I think we should have some before lunch."

Assuming bottled water and Gatorade were both out of the question, I declined politely.

The bartender then looked across at me, smiling. "Oh come, young man! Here let me pour you a glass of our good stuff. You just have to try it . . . and if you don't like, you don't drink anymore!" She started pouring a bottle of ouzo over a tall glass filled with ice. Then she poured two more—one for the man and one for the girl.

After she handed them to us, the fat man raised his and said, "Yamas!"—Greek for cheers. I raised the glass near my lips, but didn't sip any—if nothing else I wasn't going to allow them to charge me for drinking. They didn't seem to notice.

The fat man then exclaimed that the three of us—meaning himself, the girl, and me—should go take a seat in one of the red vinyl-covered booths in the corner of the otherwise empty bar. I turned to him and said, "Hey, what about lunch? You said we were gonna go to a sidewalk café for lunch."

"Oh come on, we won't take long here . . . just a couple of drinks." Now it was a "couple" of drinks. As if to entice me further, he continued, "And I have a cell phone with me I use to call my son. You can use it to call home if you'd like."

Holding the glass of ouzo, I just gave him an icy glare. As we walked to the booth I took the time to assess the situation. At the moment I only saw the man and the two women. But I had no way of knowing who else could have been in the back. I also had to assume someone had gone behind us and locked the door. I was angrier with myself than at the three visible con artists. I couldn't believe I'd been snared. I had to give it to the fat man though—I sure as hell hadn't been on the lookout for old men wearing Burberry scarves.

In such a compromised position, I'd never wanted more than to be in the U.S. Army. As a backpacker I was ashamed at having been tricked, but as a soldier I felt somehow dishonored for having been confused for a "regular" tourist.

As we sat down, the bartender asked if she could take my coat. "No thanks," I said. "We won't be staying here too long." She just smiled and nodded. I pulled in next to the fat man behind a table. Then the girl sat next to me. *Rusty! Rusty! Rusty!* I realized that I'd allowed them to pin me in.

The girl started making small talk with me—really small talk, because her English was horrible. I noticed that she wasn't even that attractive for bait. The fat man pulled out his phone and said he was going to adjust it so I could call home.

At that point I'd had enough. "Look," I said, "I've gotta go. If you'll excuse me."

The bartender saw me making my move and walked over to the table, cutting off my exit. For the first time I noticed how tall she was. She said, "You're leaving us so soon?"

"Yeah, I gotta run. Sorry. I'd love to stay."

Then she said, "Okay, hold on . . . let me just get the check."

For a brief moment I thought that maybe this would be all right. I would be willing to pay for the one drink just to call it even. That would be the cost of my stupidity. She came back and handed me the slip of paper. It was a regular bar or restaurant check, and on it she'd written beside each other a one, a two, and a five. One-two-five. I thought about that for a second. Depending on where the missing decimal point was supposed to go, I had a two out of three shot at being okay. Twelve and a half euros for a glass of ouzo would be pretty steep, but whatever.

I looked up and smiled at her, reaching for my wallet. She returned the smile, menacingly. Keeping it low so none of them could see the contents, I pulled out a five-euro bill. At the same time I scanned the rest of the bar looking for any other human movement. There was nothing.

I handed her the five euros. Without moving a muscle she looked at it and laughed. "What is that?"

"It's five euros," I said. "For the one euro, twenty-five cent glass of ouzo."

She stuttered condescendingly, "Wh . . . th . . . that's a bottle of our best ouzo. And I opened it for *you*." She was still halfway grinning.

I said, "Well okay . . . then you can keep the change."

She threw her head back and laughed.

"That's all I've got. Sorry. Take the five or leave it." I wasn't sure where I was going with this.

"Well what about a credit card?" she asked, her eyes narrowing as she began to hover over me. "You owe me one hundred twenty-five euros."

"Nope," I said, as I further veiled my wallet from view, hiding my two credit cards. "You think I'd walk around Athens with a credit card?" I continued to look beyond the tall woman, still trying to determine if there was anyone else in our presence. I put my wallet back in my pocket.

I looked away from her and glanced at the glass of ouzo sitting on the table in front of me. A grin began to tug at the corners of my mouth. The fat man on my left was starting to get fidgety, while the blond girl sitting on my right continued to smile at me hopefully. I figured she was probably getting a healthy cut out of this whole thing. The tall woman was still hovering over me, probably wondering if this budding smile was a good sign. What she couldn't see—what she didn't want to believe—was that there was no laughter behind those eyes.

I looked at the glass of ouzo again. Out of the side of my right eye, I took another notice that the seats on which we were sitting were red vinyl. *Red vinyl seats in a bar are* always *shady*. I started wondering just how serious this was—being pinned in behind the table, with my back to the wall. I guessed that my life could have been in danger, depending on how I handled the next few seconds. *There is no way to know who else is in this building.*

I looked at the glass of ouzo again. I noticed the dim light glinting off the ice cubes floating in the liquor. *What would Jimbo do?* I watched a drop of condensation slide down the side of the glass and then I made my decision. *They're bluffing. I'm all in.*

I reached for the glass with my right hand and picked it up. I said, "Okay. All right . . ." I looked at the fat man and nodded, as if I were about to take a drink. He only briefly made eye contact with me—and he looked decidedly nervous. I looked at the tall woman with a full smirk now. She looked a bit relieved—and also a bit pleased with herself for potentially being able to intimidate me into taking the drink. She knew that I was about to bring it up to my lips. She blinked, and instead of seeing me, she saw a dollar sign sitting in front of her.

I raised the glass. Then, using my hips, I pushed the table away and stood up. For an instant, she wanted to stand her ground—but then she took half a step back. That was all I needed. One last look at the average-looking blond girl, and I launched the glass of ouzo across the otherwise empty room and into the far wall. It shattered, leaving a large wet ouzo mark dripping down the wall.

The fat man and the blond girl no longer existed as far as I was concerned. I could feel them wilt in the presence of aggression. I could *sense* it. In a final fleeting look at the two still seated, *I see an average Iraqi father and daughter—confused and terrified after we've kicked in the door to their home. They look completely overpowered. They are stunned, and frozen.*

Again, the woman looked as though she wanted to hold her ground—as if this had never before happened to her. She stammered quickly that she was going to call the police.

I responded, "You call the fucking police."

Then she looked me dead in the eye. She knew then that I was serious. She stepped back, surprised and now uncertain.

I moved as nimbly as I could between the table and the woman. As I passed her, I realized that I was actually the taller one. I looked down at her without emotion. I had gone blank. I considered killing her then—right there, in front of the other two, but decided instead just to grab my coat and scarf and to be on with it.

On the way up the stairs, toward the door, the thought crossed my mind that they still could have locked me in—and that the Brute Squad in the back room, could be gearing up with brass knuckles and chains at this very second. With each step that idea concerned me a little more.

I could see daylight through a small pane of glass on the door at the top of the stairs. With each labored step I expected to hear them call for me to stop. I reached the door and turned the handle. It opened, and I walked out onto the bustling Athenian street. I quickly wrapped my scarf around my neck and threw on my black coat. With my heart racing, I walked quickly away.

For months I'd been downplaying the fact that I was a soldier. My hair was long, I had a scruffy shadow, and I liked to go on rants about how stupid the invasion had been. But I couldn't avoid it now. Turning the tables on the near-robbers had spelled such *satisfaction*. I had been parched—my veins constricted and starved of adrenaline—for months after quitting the war cold turkey. In the bar it had come back in a drenching torrent, bringing back color and sound—bringing everything back to life, all in an instant. I had been completely *comfortable* with having had my back against the wall—literally. It hadn't been a tourist in there that had thrown the glass and contemplated killing—it had been a soldier. A soldier alone, without an army.

As the feeling subsided, I lamented that while a part of me wanted it, they might *not* ever just be mountains again—that in all probability, they would always be the Hindu Kush when I looked at them. And I would probably never be the person I was before the war.

"The argument that oil's not worth fighting for . . . or that you shouldn't go to war for cheap oil—that's the stupidest thing I've ever heard." A U.S. Air Force vet was making the case in the heart of Cairo's old section.

Since he was of Middle Eastern descent, I thought maybe he had some sort of a moral authority on the subject. I was eating dinner at a kebab restaurant in the Khan el-Khalili bazaar with some Americans I'd met earlier in the week. After two months of traveling, I'd finally made my way back to the Arab world. And I did feel normal there—like that was where I was supposed to be.

"Oil's pretty goddamn important if you ask me," he continued. "Our whole fucking economy is based on it. Our whole way of life is designed around easy access to oil."

I was skeptical and thought I was listening to an industry lobbyist. But then he made his point.

"You know," he said, "if only a few countries had fresh water and they didn't want to share it, or they wanted to jack up the prices, don't you think we'd have a real gripe with 'em? Don't you think it would be worth fighting for?"

I said, "Yeah, but, I mean, water's water. You can live without oil."

"Yeah, you can live without oil, but then how the fuck are you gonna get home from here? What are you gonna to do for a living in a non-oil-based economy when you get there? No cars, no planes . . . you gonna be a farmer? And plow a field? Oil is the single most important resource we have. And it belongs to everyone. Just because it happens to be underground in a few select countries, it doesn't make it their oil. It's the world's oil."

He was on a roll. "I say hell yeah we give a hard time to the countries that want to control the market or destabilize the market." Then he tacked on: "And I'm a Democrat."

I wasn't sure where his argument stacked up in current scholarly geo-political circles, but in a strange way it made sense. Oil is pretty goddamn important.

This is the world we live in. In our world, oil is pretty goddamn important.

Home had become a strange, foreign place to me, but I didn't really have a choice in whether or not to go back. My parents couldn't understand why I was staying away; my friends couldn't figure it out either. I had tried so hard to make it home in one piece, and now I was voluntarily avoiding it. I didn't know what I was doing. Even when I remembered the times when I would have given anything to be home safe, it didn't register. When I thought about going home my head filled with static. I didn't know how to allow myself to be safe anymore. I couldn't let the damn thing go.

But outside a shady street café in Cairo one afternoon, I realized that if I were going to live like that, then the RPG might as well have flown off the launcher in Tal Afar. The bomb might as well have exploded in the valley. The result would have been the same.

On the long, westward flight across the Atlantic I started dozing and thinking, in that uncomfortable, half-asleep, upright position. I was thinking about the person I had once been. Leaning my head on the window, officer school started replaying itself on a reel in my head.

I look up from my bunk where I'm polishing my boots and roll my eyes. Cadet Moore is yelling for us to get outside for a formation. He's screaming the order, red-faced and disheveled. He looks like he's just gotten the smoking of his life. I wonder what he did. I wonder why this looks like it's going to involve me.

Ten minutes later I am still in the push-up position, sweat rolling down my nose and forming a dark spot on the dusty ground, when the sergeant calls the platoon to attention.

I close my eyes and exhale before popping to my feet smartly.

Master Sergeant Taylor is glaring at us. "Cadets, you are out here for one reason." He pauses for effect. "Your peer has left his weapon unattended. And I found it." He is trying to make eye contact with as many cadets as he can.

After his gaze passes mine, I roll my eyes.

"This is why you are being punished," he continues. "This group," he says, referring to us, "does not seem to understand the significance of this act—this negligent care for your personal weapons." He pauses

again. "This weapon is the single most important thing in your life. One day . . ." he stops abruptly, as if he has just remembered something, his gaze becoming distant. "One day . . . one of you standing here will have your life saved by this weapon." He holds it up in front of him.

I think to myself, yeah right, Mister Desert Storm/ Mogadishu-man.

He's from a different era. He's such a hardass that he doesn't realize none of us will ever actually get the chance to use a weapon in self-defense.

Then he repeats himself, measuring each syllable out carefully. "You mark my words. One day, one of you will have your life saved by this weapon. And you will thank me for teaching you how to use it." He is eyeballing a cadet in the first rank. I am still sweating, my arms still tingling from the push-ups.

I see that he is in earnest and I almost feel bad for him. He's not talking about our future—he's talking about his past. He is somewhere else, in some far-off land—talking about situations that will never come about again in our lifetime. And it means something to him. I see now that this man can in no way relate to us.

I am a cadet. It is 1999. And I know that it will always just be a misguided, boyish dream—me saving my own life with a gun, in a war.

Epilogue

A man's got to know his limitations.

Sometimes I think everything I've lived since the war is a dream. Like I'm watching my life from the outside, as if it were someone else's. There are days when I think *(know)* that the bomb that landed on my platoon really exploded, killing us all. It makes me think that what I've lived in the time since is just something my mind has conjured in that instant between the detonation and the void.

Because of this, I hold on too tight. I am too controlling, too serious. There is an urgency and desperation in everything I do. I am trying to do as much as I can in this extended split-second before that bomb bursts. I wish this moment would last forever.

Killing is wrong, war is miserable. I miss being a soldier. I cannot reconcile these things.

O'Brien explained it best to me over the phone about a year after we got back from Iraq. He was in Boston, I was in Dallas, and we were both out of the Army. He had despised the job as much as anyone—the two deployments, the combat, the infantry, everything. He always said that he'd wished he'd just stayed in the landscaping business. But in the end, on the phone, I asked him if he was still bitter about the whole ordeal.

He said of course he was. And then, in his Boston accent, he added, "Yeah, it was miserable . . . ya know . . . prob'ly the wust period of my life. I wouldn't eva do that shit again in a million yea's." I agreed.

Then he paused. "But ya know . . . we did have a pretty good time, didn't we?"

A lot of people can't understand a contradiction like that. But we can. We are enlightened.

Acronyms

ACP: assault command post
CP: command post
FARP: forward area refueling and rearming
    point; "farp"
GPS: global positioning system
ICOM: intercom; handheld radio; "I-com"
IED: improvised explosive device; roadside bomb
KIA: killed in action
LZ: landing zone
MRE: meal ready-to-eat
NCO: noncommissioned officer
NODs: night observation devices; "nods"
PT: physical training
QRF: quick reaction force
RPG: rocket-propelled grenade
RTO: radio-telephone operator
SAW: squad automatic weapon; "saw"
TOC: tactical operations center; "tock"
UXOs: unexploded ordnance
XO: executive officer

Acknowledgments

I could not have succeeded as an officer or as a writer without the assistance of a great number of people.

On the Army side, I will be forever indebted to the NCOs who taught me not only how to be a soldier and an officer in time of war, but also the life lessons that go along with that kind of responsibility. They are Jim Collins, Steve Croom, Vincent Cuevas, Chuck Nye, Rudy Romero, and Timothy Lindsey.

However, it is the soldiers who served in my platoons in combat who truly made this story possible. They were the finest soldiers I could have ever asked for, and it was a privilege to serve with them. From 1st Platoon, Bravo Company, they are: Brian Bailey, Luis Barajas, Bryce Beville, Jason Boudreau, Chad Corn, Andrew Creighton, Anthony DeGhetto, Rito Diaz, Eric Divona, Thomas Dougherty, Michael Dufault, Kwesi Hector, Kyle Johnson, Terrance Kamauf, Brant Krueger, Jose Limon, Josh Nantz, Ryan Lowe,

Christopher Morton, Peter O'Brien, Roger Paguaga, Joseph Pascoe, Craig Redmond, David Reid, Michael "Doc" Rojas, Timothy Rush, John Smerbeck, Nolan Speichinger, James Taylor, Kyle Walter, and Tony Wickline.

From 3rd Platoon, Delta Company, they are: Jesus Aguilar, Nick Ashley, Alex Estrada, Thomas Hemingson, Randell Jacobs, Matt Krueger, John Lombardo, Brandon Moose, Eric Poling, Carlos Torres, Michael Whipple, James Worley, and Trent Wykoff.

From Bravo's headquarters section they are: Reggie Garner, Ryan Kuykendall, Roger Shields, and Peter Sprenger.

I am also grateful to Captain B. and Mike Jones for having faith enough to allow me to lead my men as I saw fit. For their friendship I thank my comrades Mike Bandzwolek, Phil Dickinson, Sam Edwards, Shawn Graff, Rich Ince, Lauren Makowsky, Brian Payne, Clay White, Jim Willette, and Jason Wimberly.

On the book side, I offer deepest thanks to Dr. Michael Leggiere of Louisiana State University in Shreveport. Mike not only taught me the art of writing, but he has since continued to mentor me as I hone the craft. Without his urging, this book would never have been written.

I wish to express my sincere gratitude to my agent, Jim Hornfischer, for working tirelessly to find this book a home, as well as to Richard Kane at Zenith Press for taking a chance on it. And I'd like to thank Steve Gansen for spending more hours than he should have explaining the fine art of editing to me over the phone.

I would like to thank my friends and family for reading and rereading the manuscript. They continually offered superb advice. For any errors of fact, interpretation, or omission throughout the book, I am solely responsible.

Last, but certainly not least, I thank Sash for her unending love and support. Without her patience and understanding, this would not have been possible.